BOYS & GIRLS
JUDO
& SELF-DEFENSE

ROAD TO BLACKBELT

WRITTEN BY HAL SHARP

DISCLAIMER

Please note that all material contained in this manual is provided for informational purposes only. Martial Arts training is a potentially dangerous activity. Before beginning any Martial Arts training or exercise program, you should consult your physician. Bumps, bruises, scrapes, scratches and soreness are commonplace, and most students will encounter this sort of minor injury from time to time in their training.

More serious injuries are possible, including sprains, strains, twists, cramps, yet injuries of similar magnitude, and students can expect to encounter these infrequently.

The possibility of more serious injury exists, including fractured bones, broken bones, and torn ligaments, though rare. As with any physical activity, there also exists the remote possibility of crippling or death. In order to avoid injuries student should practice under the supervision of a qualified black belt instructor and at a club/dojo with safety equipment such as mats.

You should always be aware that if you engage in any Martial Arts course you are doing so entirely at your own risk (as described in the Doctrine of Assumed Risk and Liability), including any present and/or future physical or psychological pain or injury that you may incur. The "Hal Sharp Judo Teachers Foundation" (hereafter, referred to as the Foundation), any of its affiliates such as USJA, any contributors for YouTube videos or articles contained herein, cannot assume any responsibility or liability for any injuries, losses or third party legal actions that you may incur as a result of acting upon any information provided by this manual or any links to sites found herein.

See YouTube USJA - *Hal Sharp's History*

Hals Study of Judo in Japan

 www.youtube.com/watch?v=B5B39yYPIlQ

ACKNOWLEDGMENT

The *Hal Sharp Judo Teachers Foundation*, referred to as the "Foundation" initially prepared this manual to supplement the USJA Junior Promotion System. The manual has evolved into a complete generic judo text suitable for promotions in most organizations up to the rank of Shodan (1st degree black belt). In areas difficult to describe the instruction manual has included YouTube videos. These videos will make the manual a virtual living document. The manual is highly illustrated containing over 200 pages, 31 YouTube videos (over five hours), a practical Japanese/ English dictionary and a useful summary of current IJF contest rules. Sid Kelly, 8th Dan, prepared the dictionary.

Most of the illustrations and descriptions in the manual were based on the book, "Judo da Coloare," written by Bruno Carmeni, 8th Dan, Italy. USJA is grateful for the permission of sensei's Aida and Bruno Carmeni to reproduce their book. Our art director Eric Nishioka, changed the artwork to include girls and be multi-ethnic so as to be representative of all juniors students. We thank Sensei John Moe, 5th Dan, and his Discover Judo Club for assisting us in making these videos. In addition, we are grateful for permission to use artwork from "Boy's Judo" by Cook Hadly and Harold (Hal) Sharp, and judo artwork by William Nauta. Our author is Hal Sharp, 9th Dan, who has over 60 year's judo experience. Hal has been the co-author of the books, "Sport of Judo", "Techniques of Judo" and "Boy's Judo". Also, he has produced numerous DVDs on classic Judo and modern competitive judo. See "YouTube USJA Hal Sharp's History" to understand Sensei Sharp's judo background. Last but not least, credit must be given to Gary Goltz, 7th Dan and President USJA for his encouragement and guidance in creation of this manual.

The Foundation was established as a nonprofit affiliate of USJA for the purpose of developing educational material and programs. Most of it's funds will be dedicated for the purpose of supporting USJA and USJA/ USJF Grassroots development programs.

Contents

How to open a Youtube using an E-Book version

Click the cursor on the QR barcode

Using a printed book version

1. For use with a smart phone or tablet camera, download a free copy of the QR reader app.

    -or-

2. Search the YouTube USJA Channel, then scroll through the videos until you find the title you want.

Using A QR Code

1. Download QR Code reader application to your phone

2. Open application and take picture of the code

3. Your phone will be automatically directed to the YouTube page where the video is

Photo From http://www.fresco.co.uk/tag/qr-codes-on-banners

YouTube Contents

See YouTube USJA - *Introduction to Judo*

www.youtube.com/watch?v=jGu1TPWUJms

INTRODUCTION

This is a complete judo instruction manual for kids and instructors. The book makes judo fun for kids by incorporating games, drills and by using technical drawings with cartoons. For the older students there are excellent technical descriptions of fundamental skills needed in free practice and competition. YouTube videos are used for areas difficult to describe by text and illustrations. The use of YouTube videos make this a living manual. Self-defense is described to keep you out of trouble and how to use judo techniques if attacked. Included is a practical description of the IJF contest rules. In addition there is a dictionary of judo terms in Japanese and English with separate sections for use in the dojo, competition and techniques. This book provides a "Road to Black Belt" for both junior and senior novices.

Emphasis has been placed on the "Circle of Skills" needed to successfully make your techniques effective, such as chance/opportunity, body movement, controlling opponent , gripping, breaking opponents balance, positioning your body, effective throwing action, defense, countering, combinations and developing your skills with and without a partner.

Some ask, why should students learn many techniques? Is it not adequate to just know a few techniques and be strong, in order to beat another kid in competition? These are valid questions in today's environment.

The answer is the reasoning behind Kano's creation of judo. In order to develop a complete and confident person, he surmised that practicing a variety of skills, right and left sided, standing or on the mat, a person develops a well-rounded body and mind. You cannot predict what an opponent will do or unknown circumstances. Neither you or your opponent are the same at any time. With familiarity of many techniques, a clear mind, strong body and confidence you can overcome whatever problem may come your way. Becoming a champion is a moment in time like the blooming cherry blossom (Sakura) which quickly blossoms and fades away. That is why the Sakura symbolizes the life of the young samurai. A well-adjusted person will have a better life contribute to a better society.

In the big picture, judo will have more value if it is recognizably accepted by the general public. We need judo to grow, increasing the number of clubs and students. Judo needs to be an attractive and intelligent activity that will attract more people and have public support. To accomplish this we need to develop teachers and a well-thought-out judo education system. Hopefully, this manual with its illustrations can be useful in recruiting new players so that they can readily understand what judo is. It is important to let potential students and their parents know what is involved in judo before signing them up. For this purpose we have also provided a video that they can see on "YouTube USJA Introduction to Judo".

HISTORY OF JUDO

For almost 2,000 years Japan had little contact with the outside world. During this time there were many civil wars. Because of these wars there developed the samurai, who were the knights of Japan, and their way of knighthood (Bushido). The samurai were important men in the development of Japanese civilization. They were strong, patient, benevolent, honest, sincere, and had the courage to do what had to be done regardless of their own lives. The training included calligraphy (artistic Asian writing), philosophy, and military arts such as tactics, horsemanship, swordsmanship, archery, staff and spear fighting, and barehanded combat (jujutsu). Also, women in the samurai families adopted the samurai way and trained in martial arts. Modern judo was developed directly from jujutsu or sometimes called jujitsu.

In the old days there were no books or films. Instruction was passed down by teacher to teacher, and sometimes by the use of scrolls. Instruction from old scrolls can be seen in "YouTube USJA Old Jujutsu Scrolls."

JIGORO KANO

See YouTube USJA - *Old Jujutsu Scrolls*

www.youtube.com/watch?v=MaDnyl4H2gs

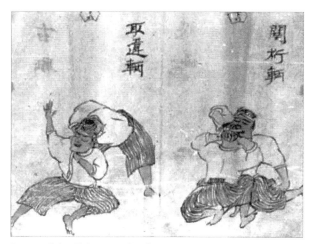
Picture of the Old Jujutsu Scrolls

Samurai started their training of young boys and girls. Today's boys and girls are tomorrow's men and women, and so this book is written to help today's youth grow into tomorrow's knights. When the doors of Japan opened to the Western World, Japan began to change and her army became modern with guns, canons, etc. The need for ancient fighting arts grew less important. During the late 1800's, a skinny student named Jigoro Kano was tired of being bullied. So he studied jujutsu. As a result he grew stronger physically and mentally. Kano thought like an educator and felt this type of activity would be beneficial to both individuals and his country. In 1882 at the age of 22, he became a jujutsu master. He then gathered the finest of the jujutsu teachers who together, developed the art and sport of judo. As a sport, judo only uses throwing, holding, choking and armlock techniques. All other arts such as striking and twisting of the wrists, legs and spine are considered too dangerous to practice as a sport. Do not think that this made judo weak. It became stronger because of the actual competition in free practice (randori) and tournaments (shiai). As a sport, judo is primarily practiced by juniors. Judo is sometimes called a physical form of chess. Kano stated, "The purpose of judo is to perfect oneself physically, intellectually and morally for the benefit of society."

Kano felt that self-defense should be an important part of judo. Through the use of katas (prearranged techniques) he kept self-defense techniques alive. Since most of these techniques were antiquated, Kano requested that Kenji Tomiki ,an aikido and judo sensei, develop a form of modern self-defense for judo. After World War II, Tomiki developed "Kodokan Goshin-jujitsu" , a modern self-defense system.

MODERN KNIGHTHOOD

Judo is a form of knighthood training. The knowledge you gain will make you a strong, confident and self-controlled person. To be a bully is to be weak. To be quiet, calm, attentive and consider ate is to be strong. When you are in trouble you must clear your mind quickly so that you can do your best. This takes much practice. It is too late to learn when trouble comes. If you try to learn judo only to hurt others, your mind is not clear and chances are you will be defeated. The goal of judo is to help make for a better society by development of well-adjusted individuals.

A NEW OLYMPIC SPORT

Judo has taken its place among the other recognized amateur sports. Internationally, judo grew rapidly. The first World Judo Championships were held in 1956 and 1958 in Tokyo, Japan. In 1960 judo was accepted by the International Olympic Committee for the next Olympic Games which started in 1964. Since then judo has grown into one of the largest sports in the world. The International Judo Federation (IJF) was formed which sets the rules for international judo championships. These rules have been adopted by all participating countries.

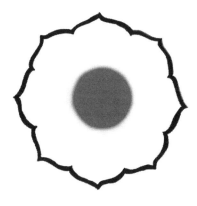

Kodokan Judo Logo

IJF Logo

KODOKAN VERSUS IJF

In the last few years the IJF has been modifying its contest rules in order to make judo more attractive to the public and keep its standing as an Olympic sport. This has resulted in eliminating various judo techniques or skills acceptable for contest purposes. Although, a player can be penalized for applying any of these techniques, it is not the intent of the IJF to eliminate these techniques from judo. In a memorandum dated 1/27/2013 the IJF stated,

> "Some may feel that this is an attack or an attempt to make extinct a specific class of judo techniques. We ask you to keep in mind that – although some of the rule changes over the last few years have eliminated some techniques from contemporary contest judo – there is nothing to prevent you from teaching those techniques to your students and allowing use of the techniques during randori or other dojo activities."

Therefore, the full range of Kodokan judo techniques are included in this manual.

To illustrate some of the French teaching methods see Youtube USJA - *French Beginner Drills*

www.youtube.com/watch?v=K1BT6mt9EpM

TRAINING JUNIOR JUDOKA

The challenge in training judo students, either senior or junior, is teaching them when they only practice on average twice a week after a full day of activity. Lecturing or demonstrating is often not effective. The student learns best when they themselves can demonstrate the subject. C.R.Rogers, a famous psychologist, stated, "The best knowledge that affects one's behavior is that which he himself has found and claims ownership too." Rogers pioneered the concept of student – centered learning. The sensei really wants the student to learn judo skills, yet the challenge is for you keep the student interested and motivated.

The French judo Federation (F.F.J.D.A) introduced a new teaching perspective for students in the 6-9 year-old range by the use of games and drills. The following are selected quotes from the French manual.

"A learning situation is an active discovery of a solution to a problem and not just the mimicking of a demonstration. An example is newaza : Instructor demonstrates a turnover, the students now do likewise. This is a demonstration copy. This time the instructor asked the students to figure out a way to turn over and pin the opponent. From amongst the solutions the student selects the best one. He may or may not add his own key points, but the students have taken an active role in finding a solution. What is important is that the students take an active role in the learning process. Progress is slow at first so be patient."

"Game Mode: Kids have a difficult time with uchikomis repetitive moves that they are unable to find immediate benefit in. Games on the other hand if devised to meet specific moves, are more readily accepted."

"Warm-ups – Calisthenics: Adult warm-ups revolve around warming the core temperature, cardiovascular system, flexibility, agility, and muscular strength. Not so with children 6-9 years of age. Here an understanding of lateral movement, kinesthetic awareness, hip movement, special awareness and rhythm are of primary importance."

"Repetitive drills versus games: Children 6-9 years of age have little concept of short or long-term goals. Their world is more immediate and requires a game type setting. Attention spans are short but are willing to explore new skills at this age. Nonetheless this group has a difficult time understanding that repeating a movement over and over again builds neural pathways that enhance quick and precise movements. This understanding develops at the later age around 14 or 15."

See YouTube - USJA *Getting Started*

www.youtube.com/watch?v=SUiats7zCBE

GETTING STARTED IN JUDO

At the beginning of judo the first things you learn are how to show respect by bowing, warming up exercises for strengthening and flexibility, and how to fall safely. To supplement our instruction we have provided you with the video of sensei's Kobayashi and Tsukamoto which were filmed in the early 1950s.

BASICS

BOWING (REI)

Bowing is the Japanese custom of showing respect like the handshake is in the Western world. In Judo we bow when entering or leaving the judo school (dojo) or the mat, to the teacher at the beginning and ending of a class and with your partner at the beginning and ending of each practice or competition. In traditional dojos a portrait of Shihan Kano is hung on the wall and at the beginning and closing of each practice session the students and sensei's bow towards the portrait. Bowing from a kneeling position is commonly practiced in Japan , it has the same significance as bowing from a standing position, however, it is considered more respectful. By being courteous at all times, you train your mind to be open and alert. Courtesy was an outstanding part of manhood training. For the development of the noble warrior, being courteous (bowing) is not just for being polite, but is also for self-defense for you must always be aware of what is around you and for being attentive.

BOWING FROM A STANDING POSITION

First we stand at attention (kiotsuke), stand straight with your arms by your side bending at the waist about 30° keeping each half of your body straight. Your hands by your side's sliding slightly to the front as you bow.

BOWING FROM A KNEELING POSITION

Starting from a standing position kneel straight down on your left knee keeping your body straight and next go down on your right knee with your toes curled under you, then cross your feet flattening them and sit back on your feet with your back straight and your hands on your thighs.

Bow by bending at the waist and placing your hands palm down making a small triangle between your fingers pointing inward on the mat. Keep your back straight and do not raise your rear end. After bowing sit up straight. Stand reverse the direction, first come up on your right leg and then your left leg.

JUDO-GI AND HYGIENE

JUDO-GI

These guidelines are primarily based on IJF rules. In competition men are not allowed to wear clothing under their jackets, like T-shirts or sweats. In Japan, at the Kodokan or other dojo's men are prohibited from wearing clothing under their jackets. In the US it is common at dojo's for men players to wear T-shirts or other clothing due to skin conditions or to lose weight. This is left to the discretion of the dojo sensei. Remember, however, that if you enter a contest with clothing under the jacket you may have to forfeit the match.

There are special rules for women as well:

"Female contestants shall wear under the jacket either: A plain white or off-white T-shirt, with short sleeves, rather strong, long enough to be worn inside the trousers, or a plain white or off-white leotard with short sleeves."

The size of the player's judo-gi is an important matter. If the player enters the mat and has an improper judo-gi the penalty will be a *Hansoku-make*, a loss. Judo-gi sizing must be checked before entering the mat. The main dimensions for the jacket and pants are that the sleeve shall cover the wrist and that the pants are not more than 2 inches above the ankle bone. The belt should not be more than 8 inches below the knot. Judo-gi needs to be clean. The IJF rules also contain more information on judo-gi sizing including limitations on patches.

OTHER RESTRICTIONS

For safety reasons a player cannot wear a hard or metallic object (covered or not). In competition this could result in a forfeiture of the match.

HYGIENE

Judo is a body contact sport and as such it is important that the individual's body and judo-gi are clean. The following guidelines on hygiene are based on the IJF rules.

(a) The Judo-gi shall be clean, generally dry and without unpleasant odor.

(b) The nails of the feet and hands shall be cut short.

(c) The personal hygiene of the contestant shall be of a high standard.

(d) Long hair shall be tied so as to avoid causing inconvenience to the other contestant.

CHECK LIST BEFORE ENTERING THE MAT

Are your feet clean?

Toenails clipped so they won't hurt anyone?

How about fingernails?

And oh yes, did you take off all of our jewelry or other hard objects that may injure you or someone you will work out with? OK?

Now we are ready.... **GO!**

HOW TO WEAR THE JUDOGI

Slippers are worn to and from the mat!

WARMING-UP EXERCISES

In judo, we bend, twist, push and pull in all directions, using all our muscles. It is important that you warm-up, so that you will be flexible and strong as a steel spring and to prevent injury to the muscles and ligaments. Warming up also enables you to move quickly and with greater power. Exercises are necessary to develop and condition muscles, especially those useful in judo, such as the legs, abdomen, neck, arms and shoulders.

WARMING-UP EXERCISES

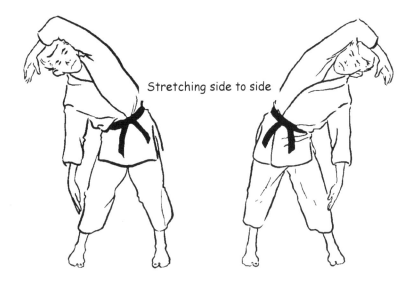

Stretching side to side

Squatting up and down with back straight and knees at 45° angles

Stretching: a) backwards and b) between legs

Squatting with person on back. Up and down action loosens top person's back

a) push-up with legs spread apart

b) Bend arms and lower body in a scooping action

c) Arch your back as you push-up

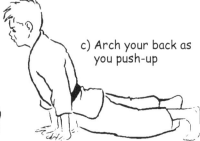

Squat on one leg and stretch the other by pushing down on the knee

Rotate head to loosen neck

Loosen ankle and toes by rotating feet

a) Stretch forward touching toes

a) Rock backwards slapping mat

a) Swing hips upward, touching mat with toes

From push-up position, switch from side to side, stepping under and through with your leg

Lock legs with partner and grip your collar. Sit up and down

FALLING (UKEMI)

Learning to fall safely will give you confidence and develop your sense of balance. Before you are thrown or throw others, you must first learn to fall. Falling is the most valuable exercise in judo. The natural things you do when falling are the most dangerous, such as reaching with your arm to stop the fall. Most people are afraid to fall or be thrown.
To overcome that fear you learn to fall safely. In judo we start you from the ground and progressively work to a standing position.

Then by cooperating with a partner, you will be thrown. You get a realistic feeling by being thrown with control, thereby mitigating any fears that you may have. In judo you learn to keep your body relaxed and slap the mat as you land in order to break the fall, this sets up a counter vibration and keeps you from reaching with your hand. You learn to fall by first sitting or lying on the mat, next from a squatting position and then from a full standing position.

When we can fall and land safely, from any position, we have removed a fear and most possibilities of getting injured. Ukemi has saved many people from broken bones or worse - so practice ukemi faithfully.

Ushiro ukemi
(back fall)

PLACH

Yoko ukemi
(side fall)

PLICH

Zempo kaiten
(tumble fall)

Curl like a ball! Pay attention to your neck, shoulder and elbow.

Rocking Chair - Fold your arms and tuck your chin in tight; then rock back and forth swinging your legs up and keeping your chin so that your head does not strike the mat. Keep legs together.

FALLING BACKWARDS

Sitting Position - Same as a rocking chair except you cross your arms in front of you and as you fall slap the mat hard with your arms along side your body. Slap as your back (beltline) touches the mat. Your arms should be approximately 30° from your body.

Squatting Position - You start from a standing position, cross your arms in front of you, squat and then fall backwards slapping the mat. Remember to keep your chin tucked in tight. Sometimes it helps to look down at your belt as you fall backwards.

Standing Position - Cross your arms in front of you, quickly squat and roll backwards at the same time slapping the mat hard with both arms.

FALLING SIDEWAYS

This is the way you normally land when you are thrown or when tumbling forward. You should practice your falls on both right and left side.

Lying Position - From your right side, place your left hand on your belt and swing your right arm across your chest and swing both legs upwards. As you roll to your right side slap the mat near your body with the right arm and let the legs fall freely. The right leg should be out straight and the left leg bent with the bottom of the left foot striking the mat. Keep your legs apart so they do not knock together.

Squatting Position - Same as a standing position, as shown below, except you start from a squat.

Standing Position - Cross your right arm and leg across the front of your body, squatting on your left leg. At the end of the swing it will fall on your right side. Slap hard as you hit the mat.

FALLING FORWARD

If you were to trip and fall with your left foot forward the natural thing to do would be to reach out which are left arm. This could injure your arm or shoulder. In this case you should tuck your left arm in and roll over your left elbow and shoulder like a hoop. You should practice your falls on both the right and left side.

Squatting position –Same as a standing position as shown below except you start from a squat with the left arm bent, touching the mat alongside your left leg.

Standing Position - Step forward with your left foot, swing your hands high above your head, palms outward. Pushoff with your left foot, tucking your head in and swinging both arms between your legs. Swing your left arm deeply inside your left foot. Roll over the outer edge of your left arm and shoulder. Slap the mat with your right arm as you land on your right side. Your landing position is like falling sideways on your right side

GAMES

Games are fun and they also provide all around training for your mind and body. Many of today's games originated from games of war practiced by warriors to keep in condition. In games you become excited and you concentrate deeply, making your mind and body work together as one. This kind of training is very important, and can rarely be duplicated in other activities. Like judo, which is a game itself, the games we play develop physical strength, sportsmanship's, confidence and respect for others.

FROG JUMPS

Team relay. Players race back and forth across the mat doing frog jumps.

CRAB WALK

Team relay. From a lying position, on your back, on all fours, race back and forth across the mat.

COCKFIGHT

Try to knock opponent down or out of the circle.

RAMS SUMO

Start is shown. Try to roll partner over or make him move outside the circle.

SIDEWINDER OR SHRIMP

Team relay. Twisting from side to side touching elbow and knee together and pushing with your feet raced back and forth across the mat.

HIGH DIVING

Individual contest. Belt is held low and each player dives over it. After each round the belt is raised a player is eliminated if he fails to clear the belt. Continue until one is left. Caution, this contest should only be done with students who have good for diving ability.

LONG-DISTANCE DIVING

Individual contest. See who can cross the mat with the least number of dives you can also have a short distance from contest. Caution, this contest should only be done with students who have good for diving ability.

SUMO

Start from a crouch. By pushing, pulling or throwing make opponent touch the ground with any part of his body except his hands or step outside the circle.

APE WALK

Team relay game. Players run on all fours across the mat. You can also imitate other animals in these relays.

DRAG RACE

Team relay. Only using your arms, pull yourself across the mat. Make sure to first turn the knot of your judo belts to your back.

See YouTube USJA - *Asahi's Tokui-waza*

www.youtube.com/watch?v=wosnhkkbw2E

LEARNING TO THROW

Throwing techniques are the most exciting part of the Judo arts. They require speed, power and split-second timing. Fighting starts from a standing position, therefore, throwing is your most effective weapon. When your opponent attacks, he uses all his strength in one direction. To defend, you initially block or avoid the attack, at the same time you take advantage of the opponent's movement and attack at the opponent's weakest point, using a smooth and complete body action.

In competition judo your opponent may be skillful and does not attack in a clumsy manner. Therefore, you must read your opponent and determine his weakest position and attack before he can change his position. In judo there are many different throwing techniques and each technique has many variations. In competitive situations, both you and your opponent present different opportunities to each other. Therefore, you must fit the technique to meet the situation. Experience will be your teacher and you will develop some favorite throws (Tokui-waza) that you will be able to use on all types of opponents and in many different situations. You first practice throwing forms by repeating it many times with a partner or by yourself until your movement is automatic and perfect.

This develops your technique and muscle memory. Then you practice throwing while your opponent moves around, still cooperating. This is like learning to ride a bicycle with training wheels. Nevertheless, you are on the "Road to Randori."

Next, your teacher puts you to the test in free practice. Your partner now becomes an opponent, does not cooperate and tries to throw you. Finally, there is the tournament where you will be nervous and challenged by a stranger. Do not worry, your opponent is also nervous about you. When you succeed in the tournament, your confidence will increase. If you lose, you will learn a lesson which still makes you a winner.

Before you learn to throw, you must learn to fall. If you are afraid to fall you will be afraid to attack, become defensive and you may not be able to throw. Remember, the best defense is an offense.

Practice throwing continuously, take your falls, improve your timing and skill, and strive to be better. There are no secrets in judo. An old Japanese poem about secrets states, "Secrets are just like your eyebrows, though they are near you, you cannot see them. When you understand a secret, you will find that it was quite near you or very simple."

ELEMENTS OF VICTORY

The Kodokan published its first book titled,"Judo Kyohan" (instruction manual) in Japanese about 1905. The book was translated into English and published in 1915 which contained about 300 pages. Covered in the book was the go- kyo- no waza (40 throws), newaza (grappling) and the atemi waza (striking). What is special about this book is that the first 100 pages were dedicated to explaining how to win in judo competition, describing the elements of victory and how the student should prepare himself. The major elements necessary to win are on the following page.

To understand the above sequences see YouTube USJA - *Elements of Victory* Demonstrated by Discover Judo Club and sensei Kobayashi.

www.youtube.com/watch?v=nJrmONxT42g

1) Opponent's position should first be broken (kuzushi)

2) Maintain your balance and be in a position to execute the throw (tsukuri)

3) In one continuous and smooth action execute the throw (kake)

NOTE:

Under the IJF contest rules you could be penalized with a" shido" for a false attack if your attack does not have an effect on your opponent, i.e. lacking kuzushi.

The book states that the tricks (techniques) will not be successful unless you can effectively set up and execute the throw as shown above. This is not as simple as it may sound. In the following sections we will describe subjects needed to succeed in throwing the opponent in a competitive environment, such as, posture, gripping, body movement, setting up the opponent, executing the throw and opportunities for throwing.

FUNDAMENTAL POSTURE (SHIZENTAI)

Samurai in former days used to pay great attention to keeping their posture free and unrestrained, not only when they were in the dojo or exercise hall, but also while sitting in their rooms. Here we can explain the attitude which one must assume when engaging in the contest. Apart from ordinary times, students of judo, especially beginners when engaging in the contest, out of fear of being thrown, are apt to adopt an unnatural posture, bending their backs, stretching out their arms, supporting their bodies with their arms, and thus placing themselves in a disadvantaged position and consequence of being thrown. With your body in such a posture, you can never move freely which makes it inconvenient for you to attack your opponent and makes you tire quickly.

You should stand erect without bending your head or body, with your feet a little separated and your knees straight. You can also modify this, especially when gripping an opponent, by standing a little bit like a boxer just slightly bent over and leaning lightly on the person. This way you can feel his body and anticipate his movements and know when to apply a throw. You should adopt a relaxed position, without being stiff, without focusing on any one thing, and with your eyes fixed 20 or 30 feet ahead. Gripping will be discussed later, however, your arms should be slightly bent and in line with your shoulders. In this position you can move freely and it will be easier to pull, push or lift your opponent. In judo such a posture is called shizen-hon-tai (fundamental natural posture). In a contest, however, you may have to change this natural posture, to an attack mode by moving one's body and arms and legs when applying a throw. When the right arm and leg are put forward we have migi-shizentai (right natural posture). And in the case of a left stance, hidari-shizentai (left natural posture). Sometimes a performer adopts a defensive posture with his knees slightly bent, his feet separated and body lowered. This is called jigotai (self-defense posture.) Such a posture sometimes serves as a means of defense and sometimes as a means to attack one's opponent who holds himself in jigotai. But when you hold such a posture you not only restrain your movements, but also tire quickly. In jigotai you cannot act quickly. If your opponent is a comparative beginner, you may sometimes find it easy to defend yourself, but in case he is advanced, you would not find it effective. (Much of the above description is adapted from "Kyohan Judo", Kodokan's first book.) Shizentai as described is more than just the physical stance, it's also a state of mind by being relatively relaxed and having peripheral vision, you have a better chance to react to the opponent's moves. This is sometimes called the" mental eye." Your center of gravity lies in your lower abdomen near the naval. This is sometimes considered the seat of power. If you breathe from your lower abdomen through your nostrils you will have greater endurance and by bringing your power up from your lower abdomen you will have greater strength. All of this is part of shizentai.

To better understand the power of shizentai, try practicing with a partner by blindfolding yourself, slightly leaning against the partner, putting your mind in your elbows. This way you will be pulling or pushing from your elbows rather than your hands. Then have the opponent attack you and you will find yourself naturally reacting to the opponents movements and stopping the opponents throws. Now, in competitive randori, practice shizentai. Once you have confidence in the ability to easily prevent being thrown through shizentai, you can stop being defensive and you can turn your attention to attacking the opponent.

An example of correct standing posture

See Youtube USJA - *Shizentai*
www.youtube.com/watch?v=RN9iHvJXuis

GRIPPING (KUMIKATA)

Gripping is one of the most important aspects of judo. When gripping, both you and your opponent can feel each other's body. There is a Japanese saying," that softness overcomes hardness." If you hold softly the opponent will not be able to feel your movements, however, if either of you hold very hard then each of you can feel other's movements. Holding includes gripping the judo-gi with your hands or hooking other parts of the body. A Brazilian Olympic gold medalist once said that the most difficult opponent he ever had was one where he could not feel where his opponent was.

In throwing it is important to control the opponent's elbow or shoulder with the pulling arm. This helps to prevent your opponent from injuring himself. Without your control he can be injured by posting on his arm or falling on his shoulder. Good control assures that the opponent will land on his back. Anton Geesink, 10th Dan, one of the worlds greatest judo champions, after seriously injuring a player in the European Championships, told me that he had learned a valuable lesson stating, "If you throw with good control, you will not only have a successful throw but a safe throw." The ultimate test of a good throw is one that works each time it's attempted in competition. At a minimum, if you have a good grip when you attempt a throw you will have control, the opponent will lose his balance, and be thrown. If you don't score an "Ippon" you will be in a good position to change techniques or enter into grappling.

Initially when students are taught a throw, they are instructed to start from a right natural position. Holding the opponent's right sleeve above the elbow with his left hand and the opponents left lapel with the right hand just in line with the opponent's armpit.

A cooperating opponent is referred to as the "uke" who is easy to throw. Sometimes the student is shown how to grip the uke by his armpits, sometimes called a "pocket grip." This is a stronger way to control and move the opponent. It is a universal grip, making it easier to throw either left or right. In his book titled "My Championship Judo,"Geesink wrote that the pocket grip was probably the strongest grip. Students are also shown other grip modifications like hooking the uke's head or around the uke's back.

Also, students should also learn to practice their throws both right and left-sided. At this stage the student learning judo is like a kid on a bicycle with training wheels. This becomes more obvious in competition, where the opponent is not a cooperating uke, who is trying to throw the student. Of course there is a lot more to throwing than just gripping, however, now we must remove the training wheels and have the student learn how to grip based on the opponents actions. Also, the student will need to concentrate on gripping the opponent closer to the elbow or shoulder for more control. In a competitive environment it can be more efficient to grip your opponent based on the opponent's actions. Trying to ignore the opponent's moves and get your favorite grip can give the opponent a chance to find your weakness.

`When gripping there is a natural tendency

KUMIKATA (GRIPPING)

With your left hand, grip the partner's right sleeve, and with your right hand, grip your partner's left collar. This is the fundamental grip for a right handed person. A left handed person does the opposite.

The standing part of judo is called tachi-waza and throwing technique is called **nage-waza**

*It is prohibited to continuously hold one collar with both hands or grab your partners belt.

to push and pull with your hands which can create a space and warn the opponent of your intended actions. Takahiko Ishikawa, 9th Dan, two- time All- Japan Champion, suggests that when gripping you put your mind in your elbows, turning your hands outwardly which helps to drive your elbows into your side. This will give you greater pulling and lifting power since you will be using your body and legs at the same time. This relates to the subject of kuzushi, the unbalancing of your oppo-

nent , which is discussed later.

The International Judo Federation (IJF) has special competition rules regarding gripping. They classify grips as normal and abnormal. Penalties are given if the player takes an abnormal grip and does not attack within five seconds. Therefore, if a tournament requires following IJF rules the player and coach must understand the rules and interpretations regarding gripping.

See, YouTube USJA- Gripping

www.youtube.com/watch?v=SVLOF596ubA

BODY MOVEMENT & CONTROL (TAI-SABAKI)

This section refers to how we walk and move on the mat. Normal walking will get you into trouble in judo because your balance will be weak. Also crossing your legs while walking is a no-no. Although there are Japanese terms for moving in different directions the term tai-sabaki is a good general term for all of these body movements. The first drill will be walking back and forth. Move forward by sliding your right foot forward with the light pressure on the ball of your foot. As you stop, you slide your left foot up to your right foot. Your left foot should be turned at an angle. At this point if someone were to pull you forward you could just slightly lean back and stop them.

When you move in this manner your center of gravity is held stable keeping you in a shizentai position. Now to step backwards you reverse the action sliding back with the left foot and then bringing the right foot back towards the left foot. Again you are now in a shizentai position. Stepping forward with the left foot is just the reverse of what we just described by stepping forward with the right foot. When you keep pressure on the ball of your foot as you step forward you can use your toes for pulling. Also you can pivot on the ball which will prevent you from twisting your ankle or knee.

For moving sideways you also do a sliding foot routine. Step right with your right foot and bring your left foot close to your right foot. You are now in a shizentai position. And the reverse when you step left with the left foot.

Next, we practice moving in circles. You could move forward with your left foot and back around with your right foot sliding your feet as you move in a circle. Backwards you can step in a circle in a similar manner. When we are doing this you are holding your opponent and moving the opponent so that you can break his balance and apply a throw. If the opponent is the one that is pushing and pulling you can use this form of stepping to follow the opponent , while retaining your balance.

 See YouTube USJA Taisabaki, which shows how this is done.

www.youtube.com/watch?v=csa8aGWJ09I

BREAKING POSTURE (KUZUSHI)

The first stage in preparing to throw an opponent is to break the opponents balance or take advantage of the opponent's movement or position which makes him vulnerable. To understand how easy it is to lose one's balance, close your eyes and slowly lean in any direction. Generally, there are two situations where an opponent's balance can be broken. First, is a two-legged man. When the opponent is standing on two legs and you pull perpendicular (90 degrees) to his stance he will come up on his toes or if you push back he will go back on his heels. The direction of your pull is sometimes called the "judo triangle." Likewise, if the opponent is standing with the right foot forward, the triangle changes direction, again if you pull perpendicular it will have the same affect. Depending on how the opponent stands there are six directions to break his balance,(1) forward, (2) backwards, (3) right front corner, (4) left rear corner,(5) left front corner and (6) right rear corner. Breaking the balance of the two- legged man is more than just pulling or pushing with your hands, you must use your whole body stepping backwards to pull and stepping forward to push. Next, we have a one legged man. Whenever a person steps in any direction, they shift their weight to one leg and the other leg is essentially off the ground. It is not possible to stand on a leg and move it at the same time, therefore, when your opponent moves any leg whether it is from stepping or attempting to apply a throw, he is standing essentially on one leg. In this situation a quick strong pull by your arm will break the opponent's balance and put him in a broken position where you can apply a throw. Of course you can also sweep the leg that is moving before it hits the ground. During competition (free practice or contest) the opponent's position is constantly changing from a one legged man to a two legged man and so forth. By using your "mental eye" by feeling and observation, read the opponent and quickly apply a throw. With a moving opponent there are two (2) more directions (sideways left & right) for a total of eight (8) directions.

Now, let's discuss the concept of "action and reaction." In the excitement of competition, the opponent with his "mental eye" can often anticipate your actions. Therefore, you try to fool the opponent by initially moving and pulling in the opposite direction first. Instinctively, the opponent will react to your action in the opposite direction thereby making it easier to break the opponents balance in the direction you intended to throw.

KUZUSHI

(OFF-BALANCING)

Just knowing the techniques is not good enough. You need to learn the basics of off-balancing as well.

Keep yourself in good balance all the time. Position yourself ready to attack when your partner is in an off-balanced postion.

EIGHT BASIC DIRECTIONS

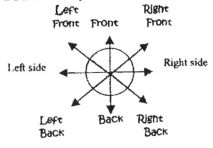

Left Front · Front · Right Front

Left side · Right side

Left Back · Back · Right Back

See Youtube USJA - Kuzushi

www.youtube.com/watch?v=2PrjrUWi9IA

POSITIONING AND THROWING (TSUKURI & KAKE)

We have already stated that before you apply your throw it is always necessary to break your opponent's posture, be at an appropriate distance and be in position to apply the throw. The former operation is called kuzushi, (to break balance). While placing yourself in a suitable position is called tsukuri (to set up the throw). As you move into a throw you cannot be too close or too far with your supporting or balancing leg in a convenient position. When both you and your opponent are in position you can at once apply your throw. This operation is what is called kake (literally applying). All of the above actions are applied in one smooth continuous movement without your opponent's awareness. When you bring it together in one smooth action it feels like nothing.

 See YouTube USJA -
Chance
www.youtube.com/watch?v=O7hRkW03qpk

 See YouTube USJA -
Takagi - Chance
www.youtube.com/watch?v=kgfllKioQ0E

 See YouTube USJA -
Tsukure & Kake
www.youtube.com/watch?v=Ao3ntdelzlQ

CHANCE-OPPORTUNITY

At this point we have discussed the various skills needed to defeat an opponent. The question now is when and how can you throw the opponent based on the opponent's actions? Here are some general guidelines:

1. Take advantage of the imperfection of your opponent's posture. For example, if the opponent is concentrating on a right-sided attack, at this point is he is open to on a left-sided attack. This is why you need to be versatile with both left and right throws.

2. Take advantage of the start of your opponents attempt to execute a waza (technique). Once an opponent has his mindset for the particular action, his mind and body become inflexible and he is like a one legged man. At this point his posture can easily be broken and thrown with a technique like Ippon-seoi-nage.

3. Take advantage of your opponent's bewildered situation. When he seems doubtful and confused, his mind unsettled, energy lacking, a mental gap is created. This typically happens when the opponent becomes defensive trying to break your grip and pulling his hand away. At this moment he is open to a one-sided throw.

4. Take advantage of your opponent if he is in a static immobile postion. In this case your opponent's mind is obstructed and will be slow to react or defend against an attack by you.

5. Take advantage of your opponent's excitement. An opponent's hurried and aggressive action may turn you on in the same way making your posture vulnerable. Avoid being dragged along with him, retain your self - control and instead dominate your opponent.

6. Take advantage of your opponent's failure to throw you and attempts to recover his balance. For example, the opponent attempts to throw you with a Harai- goshi, you block him, and as he turns to face you hit him with a leg technique such as Sasae- tsurikomi- ashi.

Note: Some of this theory was abstracted from the book titled "Kodokan Judo" by Hikoichi Aida.

UCHIKOMI (FITTING IN PRACTICE)

He is confusing speed with proper throwing skill. Make sure to come in all the way to complete a technique.

Now you must learn good Uchikomi. Uchikomi is the most important practice in judo. This is a repetition practice to learn kuzushi. Proper distance, placement of your body against uke, speed of the entry and accurcy of throwing techniques is the goal of uchikomi.

TSAAA!

See YouTube USJA -
Uchikomi

www.youtube.com/watch?v=RMVCsamaZ6A

See YouTube USJA -
French Uchikomi

www.youtube.com/watch?v=-rG35QONS1c

REPETITION DRILL (UCHIKOMI)

Kodokan defines Uchikomi as:

> *"The repetitive application of a particular technique for the purpose of learning the specific balance breaking, body shifting, power application and other technical aspects associated with it."*

Uchikomi can be practiced as either a static or moving drill. Normally this is done with two players referred to as the Tori (thrower) and Uke(receiver).

Static Drill – The Tori gets a grip, then from an appropriate distance moves in breaking the Uke's balance (kuzushi), while moving his body into the throwing position (tukuri) and simulates the throwing action (kake). Uke's role is to cooperate with the Tori, not too stiff not too soft. Tori starts to drill slowly and then picks up the pace. After 5 – 10 repetitions Tori throws the Uke. Uchikomi should be practiced on both the right and left side. If the drill doesn't feel right, the Uke should assist the Tori.

Moving drill – This is similar to the static drill except the players move around so that the Tori can get the feel of timing. This is the preferred way of doing the uchikomi because it is more realistic.

Mirror Drills – In this case the players take turns as Tori and Uke. For example, the players may pick a throw such as uchimata and then apply the throw to each other, back and forth, first slowly than picking up to speed. It is best that the players use the same technique.

Circle Drills – From a right-hand stance Tori grips Uke's collar high with his right hand and Uke's right sleeve with his left hand. Then Tori steps around in quick circles pulling the Uke in a clockwise circle. After two steps, Tori pushes Uke backward, then quickly pulls Uke forward and applies a throw. This is a fun drill. It should be practiced both left and right.

INDIVIDUAL THROWING DRILLS

Doing drills by yourself is a great way to automatically come into position when you apply a throw. For example, when doing a right side Kouchi-gari against the opponent's right leg, the student naturally reaches out with his own right leg to sweep the opponents right foot. At this point, the student is off balance. The student should have stepped in first with his right foot then brought his left foot to the back of his right foot before sweeping, this way he would be balanced on his left foot.

Individual drills for foot sweeps and other throws are shown in the referenced YouTube video for techniques such as Okuri-ashi, Deashi, Osoto-gari, Kouchi-gari, etc. These drills can be done by yourself or with an opponent.

Now as a prop we can use a stick to practice foot sweeps with. We call this the "Uke" stick. When doing these foot sweeping drills do not forget to simulate your hand action because you are not only sweeping the leg out from under the opponent but you are also breaking his balance (Kuzushi) and throwing him to the mat (Kake).

Another valuable prop is the use of bungee cords. This is superior to doing Uchikomi with a cooperating partner. Although, this can be done with a partner holding the cord, it is best to have an eye hook fastened to a wall to which you attached the bungee cord. This method works great with forward throws. You will be able to feel all of your muscles from your toes , hips and arms as you simulate a throw. If your pull is too weak or your body position is not correct then "sensei bungee" will win.

See YouTube USJA -
Individual Throwing Drills

www.youtube.com/watch?v=IzyVtot93Og

See YouTube USJA -
French Throwing Drills

www.youtube.com/watch?v=eckj3Atb-8Y

RANDORI AND SHIAI *(FREE PRACTICE & COMPETITION)*

We will also practice randori. This practice is for us to learn attacking and defending techniques without thinking who is the winner and who is the loser. It is important that we relax so that we can feel each other and learn efficient ways of using each others energy.

You are the best. Very Good! Bravo! Very fine.... Now do it again!
clap clap clap clap clap

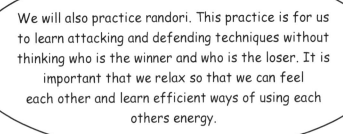

You will be able to particitpate in "Shiai" - and it is possible that the referee will grant you the victory, but you never will never know.

FREE PRACTICE (RANDORI)

Randori in judo is like sparing in boxing. It can range from soft cooperative style of practice to a competitive tournament style fight. Randori is one of the greatest parts of judo and is what sets judo aside from most other martial arts. This is the one activity that shows how skillful you are in judo. Practicing judo cooperatively is like learning how to swim on a bench, in randori you are really in the water, so don't drown.

Randori is practiced in the dojo where the players range from kids to adults, beginners to teachers. There are no losers in randori. Everyone wins as long as they try hard.

The weak try hard to beat the strong, and the strong help the weak. There is a Chinese saying, "If you are strong and powerful you do not have to show it, for your power will always be there."

In Japan at a Christmas party for a US military judo club, a Japanese schoolboy who practiced with the Americans said the following;

"In judo we show our friendship by practicing hard with each other, so when we start practice next year please be my friend and practice as hard as you can with me."

Here are three suggested ways of practicing randori:

1. **Half randori**- Similar to moving uchikomi. Here the players apply their techniques without throwing.

2. **Yaksoku (cooperation) randori**- This is where each player takes turns throwing. You can make a game out of this by having each player use a different technique than what they or the other player did, counting opposite side techniques as a different technique. Try this within a short time period (i.e.,1 minute) to see who earns the greatest number of points. A player gets 10 points for every ippon throw and five points for a week throw. If you play this game often then you will be surprised as to how many different techniques your students will learn because of the challenge that this game gives. They will study and prepare for the game. Yaksoku newaza is practiced where the players continuously move from holds, escapes, turnovers, chokes, arm-bars, etc.

3. **Competitive randori**- This is like competition except strong players have to give weaker players a chance.

If space is limited then randori sessions should be separated between throwing and grappling for safety.

See YouTube USJA
Randori

www.youtube.com/watch?v=v7uwZdUn6h4

TOURNAMENT (SHIAI)

The tournament is a real test of your ability in judo. At your dojo you'd normally compete with the same players. At tournaments outside your dojo you experience competition with other players. Competition is an essential part of judo development. Initially, you may be nervous and uncertain of yourself. It is not important to be a champion, what is important is to develop your self-confidence and improve your skills. After competition you will be more motivated to train harder and anxiously await your next competition.

Types of tournaments – Originally in Japan, a Kohaku (Red & White) style tournament was used. One player or team would wear a red or white belt. In later years, the IJF changed the coloring to white and blue, however, the term, *Kohaku* is still used for that type of contest. Kohaku tournaments were primarily used for promotion testing and team competitions. Here the players fight with the winner (Ippon only) staying to continue fighting the next and the next player. If there were no winners, the contest was considered a draw and both players eliminated. In a promotion contest a player who defeated five others the same rank would be jump promoted to the next rank, which is called a "Batsugun" promotion.

With the growth of international judo competitions, championship or elimination type tournaments became more commonplace. In this class of tournament a winner had to be decided in each match. Where there was no positive score a winner was established by the judges based on their opinion. Eventually the IJF established a complex set of rules with different degrees of scoring and/or penalizing the players in order to eliminate the use of judgment and declaring a winner.

Competition Rules – As a junior most of your competitions will be at the local level. The sponsor of each tournament can decide the rules of the tournament. For example, in some cases "drop knee seoi-nage" may not be allowed for players under 13 years of age, they may use modified IJF rules, or different weight divisions. What is most important is that you understand penalties applicable to the tournament. Most tournaments will use the IJF rules which will be discussed later in this manual.

PREPARING FOR TOURNAMENT - CONSIDER THE FOLLOWING AREAS:

-Physical conditioning

-Drilling your favorite techniques

-Study your competitors.

-Have a game plan

-Practice transitioning to the mat in case your throw is not an ippon

-Prepare yourself mentally think *"I'm going to win, I'm going to win"*

HAND TECHNIQUES

IPPON SEOI NAGE
MOROTE SEOI NAGE
TAIOTOSHI
KATA GURUMA
SUKUI NAGE

HIP TECHNIQUES

OGOSHI
UKI GOSHI
TSURI KOMI GOSHI
SODE TSURI KOMI GOSHI
HARAI GOSHI
HANE GOSHI
KOSHI GURUMA
USHIRO GOSHI
UTSURI GOSHI

LEG TECHNIQUES

DE ASHI HARAI
OKURI ASHI HARAI
KOUCHI GARI
OUCHI GARI
OSOTO OTOSHI
OSOTO GARI
KOSOTO GARI
HIZA GURUMA
SASAE TSURIKOMI ASHI
HARAI TSURIKOMI ASHI
ASHI GURUMA
OGURUMA
UCHIMATA

SACRIFICE TECHNIQUES

TOMOE NAGE
UKI WAZA
YOKO GURUMA
YOKO OTOSHI
SOTO MAKI KOMI

IPPON SEOI NAGE (ONE ARM SHOULDER THROW)

Step 1.
I provide kuzushi to uke's front

Step 2. I insert my arm very tightly under uke's armpit while pivoting in and bending my knees to get get under him...

Step 3.
I pull uke tight to my body and bow from the waist

Twisting slightly to the left as I bow, I execute the throw

A very important point for this technique is the positioning of your arm. Your arm well postioned under the uke's armpits

If tori inserts his arm without kuzushi I can choke him

Choking me! Choking me! Help!

MOROTE SEOI NAGE (TWO ARM SHOULDER THROW)

I break uke's balance to his front, simultaneously stepping my right foot in front of uke's right foot

Pivoting both feet in between his legs. I twist my right elbow under uke's right armpit

Bending my knees in order to gain leverage. I pull uke tight to my back. Bow down and straightening my legs at the same time to make the throw

TAIOTOSHI (BODY DROP)

Step my right foot to the top of the triangle while pulling the uke's body forward and upward with both of my arms to off balance my partner to the front. Then I retreat my left foot in a circular motion while pulling her body forward with my left arm and lift and push with my right arm to the uke's right. At this point, the uke is off-balanced toward her right toe.

NO

Push

YES

Keeping my right elbow at a 90 degree angle I push my partner to her right and pull her to her front. I continue the kuzushi and simultaneously straighten my right foot against the uke's right - My heel is slightly raised up I need to be upright and distribute my weight evenly to both of my feet. I Don't touch the uke's right leg at all.

I then strongly pull the uke's body downward and extend my right leg up as the uke's right leg touches my lower right leg.

SUKUI NAGE (SCOOPING THROW)
A.K.A. TE-GURM

Note: This method is a penalty under IJF rules, because the players are not allowed to touch/grab the opponent below his or her belt. After side stepping you can counter with taiotoshi.

KATA GURUMA (SHOULDER WHEEL)

From the right natural posture, I move my left foot back and pull my uke forward with both hands. As he comes further forward with his right foot, I change my left grip to his right inner sleeve and break his balance to his right front corner. Then I bend my knees and step in under him with my right foot. As I do so, I put my right arm around his right thigh and load him onto my right shoulder. I pull my left hand down toward my chest and straighten up. As the uke's weight is evenly distributed on my shoulder, I throw him down to my left front.

Note: This method of hooking the legs is a penalty under IJF rules. A modified Sode Tsurikomi Goshi could work

Position of my left hand grip

KATA GURUMA (SHOULDER WHEEL)

UP NEXT...

Koshi Waza

(Hip Techniques)

OGOSHI (MAJOR HIP)

Step 1 While I pull the uke off balance to the right front, I reach around his back and hold his body.

Step 2 Holding him tight to my body, I twist my hip across his hips...

Step 4 I bow while extending my legs hard and twist over as he goes.

Step 3 Bend my knees and place my hips below his belt

It is impossible to throw your partner unless you place your hips under your partners center of gravity. Remember to bend your knees!

To do this O Goshi well keep your body upright when you fit into your partner.

The "O" means big movement and "Goshi/Koshi" means hips

UKI GOSHI (FLOATING HIP)

Begin with the right natural posture. While turning to his right pull my uke with my left hand to make him step forward with his right foot. Then I break his balance to the right front corner by pulling a bit with my left hand. Put my right arm around his waist and step close to him, placing my right foot parallel to his, in front of his instep.

I bring my left foot back and hold him firmly against my hip. Twist my hips to throw. Pulling up on his sleeve as he falls.

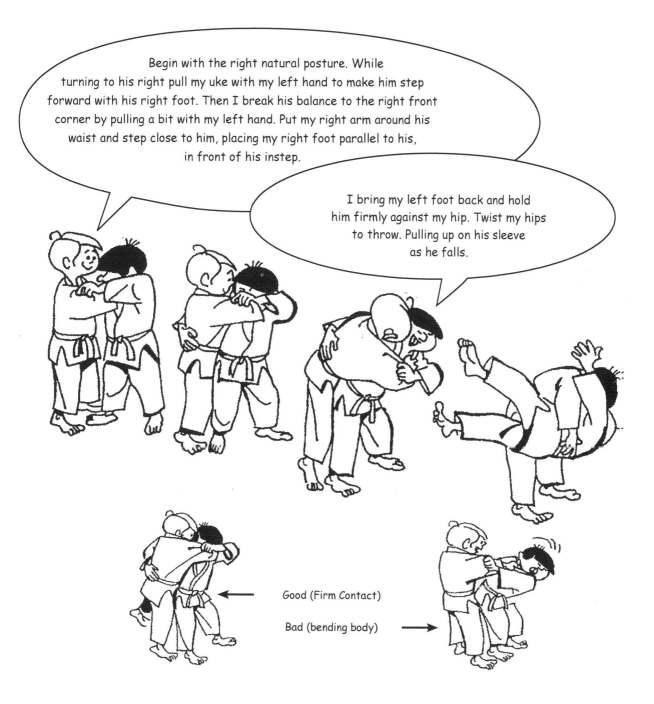

Good (Firm Contact)

Bad (bending body)

The throw differs from O goshi, in that you do not raise your hips or bend forward.

Throw with a thrusting and twisting action

73

TSURIKOMI GOSHI (LIFT-PULL HIP)

Tsurikomi Goshi is the same movement that a fisherman does when they catch a fish. A fish hook action is done with your right hand pulling and lifting opponent's left side in a circular motion. I make my uke rise up by lifting him hard while making kuzushi to his front. While holding the uke up, I fit in with a bent knee, and straight back posture.

Make sure that my hips are placed well below the uke's center of gravity, then pull my uke over my hips.

The movement of your right hand is very important. You must push high toward the ear. Don't forget to pull with your left arm.

SODE TSURI KOMI GOSHI

Sode Tsuri Komi Goshi

The Sode Tsurikomi Goshi
Is applied to the left, pushing your
opponents right elbow upward.

Similar to tsurikomi Goshi, except
you push uke's arm by the elbow and
across uke's face.

HARAI GOSHI (SWEEPING HIP THROW)

As I step my right foot near the top of the triangle, I make my uke off balance to his right front corner by pulling with my left arm and pulling lifting (fishing) with my right arm.

Then I bring my left foot behind my right foot and turn to my left to place my hips against the uke's low abdomen. I sweep his right leg from his thigh down to his ankle with my right leg.

The off balance is obtained by pulling with my left hand towards the direction of my shoulder.

Do not place your hips to deep against your uke's front or bend your leg when you sweep. You will just end up sweeping the air.

HANE GOSHI (SPRING HIP)

Break the uke's balance to the right front corner, while stepping your right foot to the top of the triangle. Bring your left foot behind you. At the same time, bend your right knee and place your leg against the inside of the uke's right leg. With your hands, pull your partner to you and load them onto your hip. Straighten your left leg and lift the uke off the mat with a springing action in you right hip and leg. Then twist to the left and pull out and down hard with both your hands. The uke should turn over your right hip and land at your feet.

KOSHI GARUMA (HIP WHEEL)

This technique is similar to O Goshi except I reach around the uke's neck rather and around his back in order to get her tight to my body

USHIRO GOSHI (BACK HIP THROW)

Ushiro Goshi is used to counter a hip throw. The Uke tries a hip throw. I lower my hips and put my left arm around his waist. While holding him close to me, I straighten my legs and bend my body backward. Then I swing him up off the mat. As he begins to come down, I move my legs back. Bend forward and pull him down to the mat so that he cannot land on his feet.

Don't forget to slap.

SPLASH

UTSURI GOSHI (TRANSFER HIP OR CHANGING HIP)

Utsuri goshi is a counter throw. The uke tries a right angle hane goshi. As he moves in, I lower my hips, grab the back of his belt with my left hand and pull him up with my arms and waist. Then I swing him to my left and twist my hips to the right. Continue sweeping him up to the left and put my left hip under him, twisting my hips to the right pulling down hard with my right hand as I continue twisting my hips to the right.

UP NEXT...

Foot and Leg Techniques

DE ASHI HARAI (FORWARD FOOT SWEEP)

You need to make your uke move forward, backward or sideways. To demonstrate, I will make him move forward

Draw your right foot back and pivot 90 degrees to the side. Pull the uke's left lapel with you right arm.

Then place the sole of your left foot, the area around the arch, against the uke's left ankle and sweep his left foot toward his left toes. Pull the right sleeve downward with my left hand to throw him.

OKURI ASHI HARAI (SLIDING OR FOLLOW FOOT SWEEP)

Uke steps to his left side. I follow him by stepping to my right. As he moves his right foot to the left, pursue it with my left foot. Just as he is shifting his weight to his left foot and starts to move his right foot to the left, sweep it with the sole of your left foot in the direction that he is moving. At the same time, lift up with my right hand and push it down with my left. The uke's legs will fly out from under him.

Oυιоυιоυιоυιоυι!!!

No No! **Okuri ashi!** not **ouchi ashi!**

For the technique to work, you must stay loose and move smoothly. Put the sole of your foot as close as possible to his outer ankle and sweep just as he is shifting his weight to his right foot Be sure to sweep with your whole leg, not just your foot. Sweep in the direction his foot is traveling.

KOUCHI GARI (MINOR INNER REAP)

This is a rear throw. I make the uke off balance to his back by pushing him backward with my right arm and by pulling his right sleeve down and towards me.

Quickly I bring my left foot behind my right heel, then bring my right foot behind his left foot and then sweep the uke's right foot from his heel towards his toe. I need to keep the outer edge of my right foot sliding over the mat surface while sweeping.

I must push the uke backwards with my entire body

I push him to the right back with my right arm.

I pull downward with my left arm

O UCHI GARI (MAJOR INNER REAP)

I step my right foot to the top of the triangle position at the same time I pull the uke downward with my arms to make my opponent off balance to her rear. Keep your eyes facing straight forward.

Bring my left foot behind my right foot and point my heel to her. Keep using my arms to immobilize the uke's upper body.

Continuing the toe circle wide your opponents' stance while driving your body forward with your left leg.

Insert my right leg between her legs and start dragging my big toe in a circle to sweep her left leg. I make contact just below the back of the knee with the same spot of my leg.

O SOTO OTOSHI (MAJOR OUTER DROP)

Note: The main difference between Osoto-otoshi, and osoto-gari, is that in osoto-otoshi, you drive your heels behind uke's leg. Whereas in osoto-gari, you reap uke's leg

Turn to the uke's right, driving him onto his right leg by pulling his right elbow in and pushing against the left jaw in a wheel motion

Hook the right leg, at the same time drive hard with your let leg using a very strong hand action.

Throw by driving you right leg down crimping the right knee pushing him into the mat.

O SOTO GARI (MAJOR OUTER REAP)

Make your partner off-balance by pulling your left hand toward your ribs and lifting him up slightly with you right hand. At the same time, you step your left foot next to his right foot. Then bring your right leg forward and sweep his right leg with force.

The action of the hand is very important. Keep your partners weight on his right heel by the lifting and pulling action of your right arm.

Basically, you do not try to catch his leg, but thrust your right leg hard and keep it straight while leaning your body forward.

Fish hook Action!

KOSOTO GARI (MINOR OUTER REAP)

First break the uke's balance to his right back corner, then reap his right foot from behind with my left foot and throw him backward. I need to place my right foot at a right angle to the uke's right foot. Ideally the sole of my left foot skims the mat as I reap, keeping my big toe raised. However it is permissible to twist my foot and reap with the sole of my foot.

HIZA GURUMA (KNEE WHEEL)

I step my right foot just outside of my partner's left foot. Make sure that my right toes are pointing toward his body. At the same time, off balance him to his right front.

Continue to pull the uke forward. I steer his upper body like I was turning a huge steering wheel.

I touch the outside edge of his knee with the bottom of my foot and block his movement. I need to keep my left leg straight. Also keep him off balance to his right front.

SASAE TSURIKOMI ASHI (SUPPORTING FOOT LIFT-PULL THROW)

As I step my right foot in front of the uke's left foot, I make the uke off balance to her right front by pulling with my left arm and pull-lifting with my right arm.

While I am keeping my uke off-balanced to her right front, I place the sole of my left foot around the arch in front of the uke's right ankle. I keep my body straight from my left shoulder to left foot while turning my body to the left and throwing my uke.

Don't bend your body

Keep my body straight from head to foot.

Tsurikomi - Fish hook action

HARAI TSURIKOMI ASHI (LIFT-PULL FOOT SWEEP)

I step forward with my left foot and make my uke step backward with his right foot. I must place my right foot close to his left, my toes pointing inward. As the uke steps his right foot back again, I break his balance to his right front corner by lifting and pulling (tsurikomi). I stretch my left leg out, and with the sole of my foot sweep his right outer ankle or shin away from me. Simultaneously I twist my upper body to my left and pull hard toward my left armpit with my left hand and push upward and toward my left with my right hand to throw him.

Tsurikomi
Fish hook action

Block - **Sasae**

Sweep - **Harai**

ASHI GURUMA (LEG WHEEL)

Step back with my right foot an when my opponent comes forward with his left, break his balance to his right front corner with my hands (left hand pulls toward his right front corner and push him to his right with my right.) Bring my left foot around behind me and pivot to the left. Stick my right leg across the uke's legs and press against his right knee cap, my ankle extends slightly past it. Draw him close to me with my left hand and continue pushing the uke to his right, with my right hand and twist to the left. Uke will rotate over my leg.

More Kuzushi!

O GURUMA (LARGE WHEEL)

I break the uke's balance to his right front corner, place my leg across his right upper leg to lower abdomen area, and lift him by swinging my right leg up and back. At the same time, pull down with both hands. The uke should turn over my leg.

You must notice the resemblance between O Guruma, Harai goshi, and Ashi guruma. You must pay attention to them and not confuse them

O guruma

My Leg is in contact with the front of his upper leg and I sweep up

Harai Goshi

My leg contacts my uke's lower leg and I sweep up

Ashi guruma

My leg blocks the uke's right knee cap and I use my hand and arms to throw him forward.

UCHI MATA (INNER THIGH)

I step my right foot to the top of the triangle position at the same time I pull uke off balance to his right front corner with my hands and arms. I bring my left foot around behind me. At the same time, I bend my right knee then I sweep his left inner thigh with the back of my right thigh to throw.

Make Sure to have good contact with your chest before sweeping your leg.

Leg Technique

Hip Technique

(Hane/uchimata)

UP NEXT...

Sutemi-Waza

(Sacrafice Techniques)

TOMOE NAGE (CIRCULAR THROW)

Step forward with your left foot and push the uke hard directly backward. The uke pushes me back and comes forward with his right foot. I move my left hand to his right lapel. While pulling him onto his toes with both hands, slip my left foot in between his legs, bend my left knee and sit back, placing my hips as close to my left heel as possible. At the same time, bend my right knee and lightly put the sole of my right foot on his lower abdomen. Push his body up by straightening my right leg, and pull with both hands to throw.

UKI WAZA (FLOATING THROW)

Step back with my right foot. When my opponent comes
forward with his left, break his balance to his left front corner. To recover
his balance, he will bring his right foot forward. Just at that moment, slide your left
foot outside of his right foot. Drop back to my left. While falling pull my left
hand in an arc toward my body and push my right side in and
arc to the left. Uke falls forward to his right corner.

YOKO GURUMA (SIDE WHEEL)

When the uke tries a right side throw stop his action by pulling him against you and stepping over his leg.

As he bends forward to throw swing your right leg through his legs dropping on your right side.

Throw by bridging with your legs and using a strong circular hand action. Your right hand catches his stomach and your left hand grabs his belt.

Right hand on stomach

Left hand on belt.

YOKO OTOSHI (SIDE DROP)

As uke steps sideways you drop down sliding you left leg across his right leg blocking it.

As you drop down, throw the uke sideways with a strong circular hand action while bridging with your legs.

SOTO MAKIKOMI (OUTER WRAP-AROUND THROW)

From the right natural posture, I break the uke's balance to her right front corner. As uke tries to keep her balance, she steps forward with her right foot, then left foot. When she is about to shift her weight to her right foot, I turn to my left and bring my left foot back around me. I put my right foot outside of her right foot and let go of my right grip, then pull her to my right side with my left hand. I continue twisting to the left wrapping her arm and body, and throw myself forward and downward

See YouTube USJA -
Block and Counter

www.youtube.com/watch?v=jfnoS2XACbc

APPLICATIONS

BLOCKING, AVOIDING AND COUNTERING

Blocking – When an opponent attempts a throw and you sense his movements by the "Mirror Eye" (visually and /or by feel) you can block his action. For example, if the opponent attempts a right side hip throw, you can counter rotate pushing your left hip forward and pulling a right-hand back. At this point by retaining your balance you can throw the opponent onto his back and go into mat work. If the opponent attacks you from the front with a leg technique, like Osoto-gari, you merely have to push him away with your hands.

Avoidance – If the opponent attempts a throw, failing to break your balance, you can simply walk into the opponent deflecting the attack. Also you can step around like a bullfighter and deflect the opponents attack.

Countering – Blocking or avoiding an attack are defensive moves. When an opponent attempts to throw he is usually shifting his weight from one leg to another and is susceptible to be counter thrown. For example, if the opponent attempts Osoto-gari, whereby he lifts his leg during the attack, by snapping the opponent into you he can easily be thrown with Ippon-seoi-nage or Osoto-gari. The timing of many throws is done by countering the opponent's actions. This will be further discussed under the subject of "Chance."

View our YouTube USJA -
Combinations, which illustrates the combination methods.

www.youtube.com/watch?v=wE8VHjUCQbA

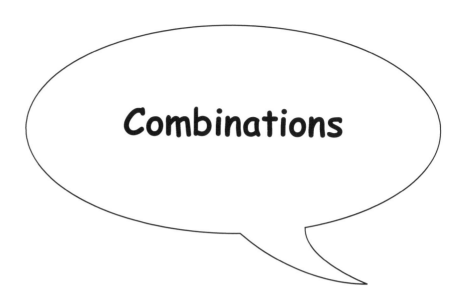

COMBINATIONS (RENRAKU WAZA)

It is best not to use a combination, but to apply to throw directly with good timing, force and speed. The downside of combinations are that you are only going partway for one throw and then changing to another without a full commitment. However, combinations are effective tools to create an "action and reaction" helping to set-up the opponent for a throw. There are several types of combinations that can be used.

1. There is the" faint," whereby you quickly simulate a throw – as you feel the reaction, apply the intended throw.

2. There is the "setup throw," whereby you lightly attempt to fake a throw and quickly move into your intended throw.

3. Then there is the "changing throw," whereby you attack full speed with a throw. As the opponent senses your action and blocks the throw, without releasing your grip, you change into another throw in the opposite direction. For example, you try a forward throw, and as the opponent pulls back to block to throw, you then switch to a backward throw catching the opponent off guard.

4. There is the "bouncing cork" routine, whereby quickly try to snap the opponent down and forward, and as the opponent resists your downward pull you quickly snap up and apply your throw. This is like pushing a cork down into a glass of water and when you release the cork it pops straight up.

5. "Tsurikomi" lift – pull action. Your driving arm moves in a circular action like a fish hook which causes the opponent to pull back in the opposite direction. This is similar to the" faint."

HIZA GURUMA TO O SOTO GARI

O SOTO GARI TO HARAI GOSHI

OUCHI GARI TO TAIOTOSHI

UCHIMATA TO OUCHI GARI

GRAPPLING TECHNIQUES (KATAME WAZA)

This is a general name for hold downs, strangles, and jointed locks used in grappling. The term newaza is essentially the same, referring to the actions taken while on the ground. Junior players under the age of 13 are only allowed to do hold downs (Osaekomi) in competition (Randori or Shiai). From 13 years of age juniors may use strangles (Shime-waza) in competition. Joint locks on the elbow joint (Kansetsu-waza) are not allowed by juniors in competition, only by black belts.

Submission techniques, strangles and joint locks, are taught to juniors for technical knowledge, and should only be used under direct supervision of the sensei.

Katame-waza is exciting and fun as the student transitions from attempted throws into mat techniques. In the dojo randori (free practice) is also practiced on the ground.

Remember, all fighting starts standing but ends up on the ground. So, the importance of throwing versus mat techniques is about 50-50.

See YouTube USJA - *Ishikawa Newaza*
Demonstration of newaza randori.

www.youtube.com/watch?v=QqOS7uE2d_U

See YouTube USJA - *Kawakami's Newaza*
Newaza entry, control and techniques.

www.youtube.com/watch?v=VEgmec91t88

HOLDING TECHNIQUES

OSAE KOMI
ENTERING INTO MAT TECH
KESA GATAME
KUZURE KESA GATAME
MAKURA KESA
USHIRO KESA
YOKO SHIHO
KUZURE YOKO SHIHO
KAMI SHIHO
KUZURE KAMI SHIHO
TATE SHIHO
KUZURI TATE SHIHO
KATA GATAME

CHOKING TECHNIQUES

HADAKA JIME
OKURIERI JIME
TBA KATA HA JIME
RYOTEJIME
KATA JUJI
NAMI JUJI
GYAKU JUJI
ASHI GATAME J.
SODE GURUMA J.

ARMLOCK TECHNIQUES

UDE GATAME
UDE GARAMI
HIZA GARAMI
JUJI GATAME
WAKI GATAME
HARA GATAME

HOLDING TECHNIQUES (OSAEKOMI WAZA)

Holding techniques are not as difficult as throwing, but they are just as important. Although most fights start from a standing position, they usually end up on the ground. When you attack with a throw there is no assurance that you will win by ippon, therefore, your action should continue into the mat to pin the opponent or apply a choke if allowed. In holding the object is to control your opponent on the ground, on one or both shoulders touching the mat, with your body in a kesa, shiho or uragatame position. Time for scoring in competition is Ippon 20 seconds, Waza-ari 15 seconds or Yuko 10 seconds. If your opponent starts to escape and you change your position moving into another hold the time will still count. In holding you should be slow and direct like a Boa Constrictor snake in order to continually control the opponent or change your position. You only need to immobilize one part of the opponent's body at one time. For example, if you hold his right shoulder he cannot move his shoulder and therefore the rest of the body cannot escape. The following are some general guidelines to working on the mat.

The following are some general guidelines to working on the mat

WHEN YOU ARE ON TOP

- Keep your body low and relaxed.

- Keep a grip on his body at all times.

- Move in slowly and steadily.

- Keep above opponents waist to avoid his legs.

- Keep your body close to his at all times.

- Only press against one part of his body at a time.

- If he starts to break a hold, shift to another hold.

WHEN YOU ARE ON THE BOTTOM

- Keep the space between you and opponent in order to escape.

- Keep opponent below your waist so that you can use your legs to control him.

- Do not allow him to obtain a hold or escape will be difficult.

- If you are held try to escape with small wiggly actions.

ENTERING INTO MAT TECHNIQUES (NE WAZA)

OSAE KOMI WAZA (HOLDING TECHNIQUES)

Judo in not only practiced standing up, but also on the mat. Lets practice holding techniques. At first, have your uke lie on his back and do not let him get up!

The name of the hold indicates the side you position yourself in. practice your techniques and learn the names

Finally it is not so difficult. These names are always the same words that we repeat. You can learn and remember them

Tt is prohibited to place your foot on my stomach, tickle, pull the hair, twist fingers, place hands on his face, bite or pull on the ears....It is illegal I say "IT IS ILLEGAL!"

KESA GATAME (SCARF HOLD)

KUZURE KESA GATAME (MODIFIED SCARF HOLD)

It is very similar to Kesa Gatame. The only difference is your right arm position. You insert your right arm under the uke's left arm.

Place your knee under his shoulder

Place your right hand on the shoulder

You can grab his collar like this...

You can place your palm on the mat and squeeze the uke's body with your hips and your elbow

MORE Varitations of Kesa Gatame

MAKURA KESA GATAME (PILLOW SCARF HOLD)

Similar to kesa gatame except slide over the uke's right shoulder putting your thigh under his head like a pillow.

USHIRO KESA GATAME (REVERSE SCARF HOLD)

This is a reverse Kuzure Kesa Gatame immobilizing the uke's right side. To control his left side grip his belt.

YOKO SHIHO GATAME (SIDE FOUR CORNER HOLD)

You lay at the side of your partner and grab his collar with your left hand. Also, you grab your partner's pant, end of jacket or belt, to hold it down

KUZURE YOKO SHIHO GATAME (MODIFIED SIDE FOUR CORNER HOLD)

Similar to Yoko Shiho Gatame, except your right arm is over his shoulder and holds the belt

Your right hand grips his left sleeve or is used as a stopper in case the uke bridges to the left.

KAMI SHIHO GATAME (UPPER FOUR CORNER HOLD)

Staying behind your uke. You cover him with your body. Place your hands under his shoulders and grab his belt, pulling him towards you. Place your head to the right or to the left. You may rest your chin on his stomach but without pushing.

Control your uke from the top of his head with 4 points of support.

You can have your knees bent or you can have your legs spread wide apart depending on the uke's actions

KUZURE KAMI SHIHO GATAME (MODIFIED FOUR CORNER HOLD)

Similar to Kami shiho Gatame, except your body is not over his head, but is at an angle over his shoulder.

TATE SHIHO GATAME (STRAIGHT FOUR CORNER HOLD)

Straddle the uke's body by hooking your knees tight against his waist with your heels under his thighs.

Trap his left arm against his head, gripping your collar with you right arm gripping your own collar.

KUZURI TATE SHIHO GATAME (MODIFIED STRIGHT FOUR CORNER HOLD)

Similar to tate shiho except you hunch forward trapping his left arm with both your arms. Grip your collar with you right hand and his belt with your left. Hook your feet under his thighs

KATA GATAME (SHOULDER HOLD)

My right forearm, my right knee and my left foot form a triangle for perfect balance.

I press the uke's arm across his face and hold it there with my neck. I also reach around under the uke's neck and grip my hands together.

DRILLS AND ESCAPES FROM HOLDS

There are many good drills in newaza. In this section we have chosen to combine drills with entries and escapes. Drills that can be utilized in holding an opponent or escaping are as follows:

1. Push-up with a step through action. You start in a push-up type position with your legs apart now bring your right leg up and shoot it across under your left leg, next pick up your left leg and shoot it across under your right leg and so forth keep going back and forth. This exercise helps you keep your balance on the ground when changing positions.

2. Push-up with a step back action. You start in the push-up type position and then bring your right leg backwards over your left and as far up as possible. This exercise is useful when you are controlling the opponent's legs and want to move up towards his head.

3. Dragging your body forward across the mat. A common drill is to reach out with your arms and pull your body forward. Although this is good exercise it is not too useful in newaza. Modify this exercise by bringing your legs up into a frog type position and push your body forward with the inside edge of your feet. This exercise is useful when you try to turn an opponent over who is lying on the stomach or in a turtle position. In this case you reach through catching the opponents elbow and knee on the opposite side putting your chest into his side and pushing with your legs to turn him over.

4. Pushing backwards with your legs while lying on your back. When an opponent is holding you with his hands under your body, this drill will put pain against his knuckles or arms causing him to release you.

5. The Shrimp or Sidewinder drill is where you learn to keep off your back and turn towards the opponent so that you can escape from his holding action. While lying on your back bring your legs up close to your buttocks, bridge on your shoulder creating a space under your back. Now quickly turn into that space so that you're lying on your side and your elbow is against your knee. Now you have the option of pushing the opponent away or reach over the opponent grabbing his belt and doing a bridge and roll escape.

6. Another shrimp type action is that when you are bridging you push your opponent with both hands up and away from you . This will create a space for you to turn out of. If the opponent pushes back against you , then you can quickly grip his body and do a bridge and roll escape.

7. A sit-up or Humpty Dumpty drill can help you escape from kesa-gatame by driving the opponent backwards as you sit up and push him backwards.

8. A wiggle-wiggle routine is useful when the opponent holds you tightly and you want to turn out to escape. Here you relax and pull your arm out as you turn in small quick jerking actions while you push him away with your other arm.

9. A reverse Kata-gatame can be done from the bottom. When your opponent tries to get a hold, like a Kesa-gatame, and attempts to reach around your head, then push his elbow against his head, place your head against his elbow and squeeze his arm and head with both of your arms. From this position you can either strangle the opponent or roll him over his shoulder.

 These drills are demonstrated in YouTube USJA-*French Newaza Drills*

www.youtube.com/watch?v=3lzqJ656-SU

 These drills are demonstrated in YouTube USJA-*Holding Drills and Escapes*

www.youtube.com/watch?v=YlGJUMUWGL0

ENTRY FROM LEGS

1. KESA GATAME
2. K. YOKO SHIHO
3. YOKO SHIHO
4. KAMI SHIHO
5. TATE SHIHO

TURNOVER

1. KESA
2. YOKO SHIHO
3. YOKO SHIHO
4. KAMI SHIHO
5. KESA
6. KATA KATAME

ATTACKING FROM BOTTOM

1. K KESA
2. K KESA
3. TATE SHIHO
4. TATE SHIHO

FREEING TRAPPED LEG

1. YOKO SHIHO
2. KAMI SHIHO
3. TATE SHIHO

THE ENTRY

There are the techniques to penetrate against the uke's defense. We will learn the basics of entry from the opponent's legs. These techniques will give you the advantage

ENTRY FROM LEGS NO. 1 (KESA GATAME)

Your opponent is on his back in front of you. You grab his ankles and you fake push them to the right. Then bring them to his left using his reaction

You place your right foot right next to the right side of his hip. Then zoom yourself into apply osaekomi.

ENTRY FROM LEGS NO. 2 (YOKO SHIHO)

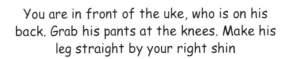

You are in front of the uke, who is on his back. Grab his pants at the knees. Make his leg straight by your right shin

Place his right leg under your right lower leg and block the uke's right leg. Then advance your left leg and grab his collar near the left shoulder and hold him with yoko shiho gatame

ENTRY FROM LEGS NO. 3 (YOKO SHIHO)

1. Grab your uke's belt and spread his legs with your elbow
2. Grab his right arm sliding your right leg over his right leg for control
3. Reach around his collar and move into Yoko Shiho Gatame
4. Tighten the hold by placing your knees in his side.

ENTRY FROM LEGS NO. 4 *(KAMI SHIHO)*

Enter between the uke's legs grasping his pants at the knees and spreading his legs. Control his right leg by sliding it to the right over his right leg.

Grasp his belt with your right hand and reach over his left shoulder with your left hand. Step around into Kami Shiho Gatame

ENTRY FROM LEGS NO. 5 (TATE SHIHO)

Take the feet of your opponent and pull them towards you and hug his knees Then crawl, as you would climb up a tree and hold him in the tate shiho gatame.

TURNOVER NO. 1 (K. KESA GATAME)

(1)Uke is in "all four position" Approach the uke from his head. Grab the uke's belt at the center of his back with your right hand. Then push the uke downward with your right elbow to keep the uke's head down. (2) Insert your left hand under the uke's left arm and pass it under his right armpit and scoop up the uke's left arm. (3) Grab the uke's left elbow area with your right hand and pull it toward you at the same time you push the uke's left side to his right, (4) Turn over and hold him down with Kuzure Kesa Gatame

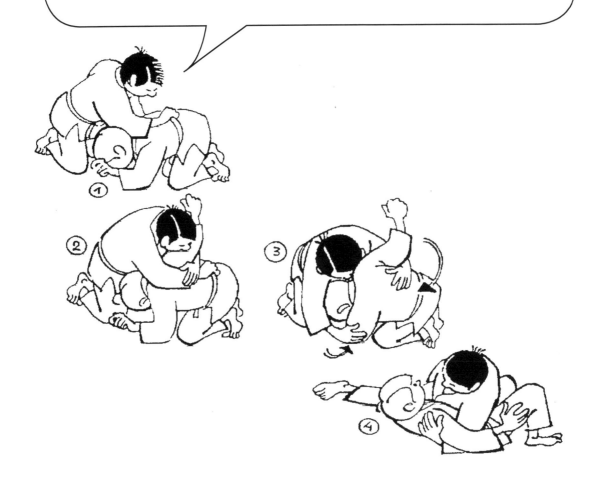

TURNOVER NO. 2 (YOKO SHIHO)

Uke is in "all four position" Approach the uke from the side. Insert your arms under the uke's body and grab both of the uke's arms and pull them toward you while keeping your chest in tight contact against the uke's left shoulder and left side of his body. Keep pulling and pushing the uke to his right side and hold down with yoko shiho gatame

TURNOVER NO. 3 (K. YOKO SHIHO)

Uke is in an "all four position." Approach the uke from the head. Insert your arms under the uke's armpits and grab both of the uke's collars. Pull the uke's left arm towards you (1). Roll your body to your right side by bringing your head under the uke's body. Continue rolling while pulling the uke's lapel with your left hand (2-3) You will find your self in kuzure Yoko shiho gatame (4)

TURNOVER NO. 4 (K. KAMI SHIHO)

Uke is in an "all four position." Approach uke's right side. Insert your arms under the uke's armpits and grab both of the uke's collars. Block the uke's right knee with your right knee and start to roll to your right and bring the uke's body to the top of your body (2), Keep controlling the uke's body with your arms and start bring your legs back towards you and control the uke in kuzure kamishiho gatame (3-4)

TURNOVER NO. 5 (K. KESA GATAME)

1. As the uke turns to his right, hook his left arm with your right arm gripping his belt with your left hand.

2. As you turn him over drop to his right side and control him with Kuzure kesa gatame

TURNOVER NO. 6 (KATA GATAME)

1. With the uke on all fours approach from his rear.
2. Reach around his waist tightly and turn him over stepping through with your right leg.
3. Falling on your right side, turn him over with your arms and body.

4. Pin uke with kata gatame

ATTACKING FROM BOTTOM NO. 1 (K. KESA GATAME)

ATTACKING FROM BOTTOM NO. 2 (K. KESA GATAME)

As uke lunges forward between your legs, pull his right arm down and hook your right arm under his left arm. Turn him over using your legs as in technique no. 1

Pin him with kuzure kesa gatame.

ATTACKING FROM BOTTOM NO. 3 (TATE SHIHO)

When uke enters between your legs, sit up pulling him in by his elbows and lifting him up and over like Tomoe Nage. Roll up and over into a Tate shiho gatame.

ATTACKING FROM BOTTOM NO. 4 (TATE SHIHO) NO.

Like Technique No. 3, except uke pulls you
forward as you grab him, then you sit up and
pin with tate shiho gatame.

FREEING TRAPPED LEG NO. 1 (YOKO SHIHO)

Need to know

1. You must control your opponents upper body. See picture 1.

2. You need to make your leg upright and bring your ankles as close to you opponent's buttocks

After I control the uke's shoulder and head, I switch my hip, similar to Ushiro Kesa Gatame and I grab my uke's pant around his left knee. I place my right leg (or right knee) against his right thigh and push it away while at the same time I pull my right leg toward me to free my right leg.

Then I control the uke with Yokoshiho Gatame

FREEING TRAPPED LEG NO. 2 (KAMI SHIHO)

After I control the uke's shoulder and head, I switch my hip to Ushiro Kesa Gatame and I grab my uke's pant around his left knee. Then I move my right arm under his left armpit and twist my hips to my left while standing on my left foot (2) I then bring my right leg over his right thigh.

I sit on my right knee and place my left foot against his right lower thigh and push it away, while I am pulling my right foot towards me.

Then I bring my left arm over his head and under his left shoulder to grab his belt with my left hand. I move myself to the top of his head and grab his belt with my right hand either over or under his right shoulder into kuzure kami shiho gatme or Kami shiho gatame.

FREEING TRAPPED LEG NO. 3 (TATE SHIHO)

After I control the uke's shoulder and head, I scoop his left arm and cover his body with mine. At the same time I bring my right knee over his left leg very near the hip joint. Place your weight on his head area then bring your left foot to the inside of the uke's right leg near the hip joint and push hard to open his leg wider so that you can get your right leg out from his legs. Control uke with tate shiho gatame.

SHIME WAZA (CHOKING TECHNIQUES)

Chocking techniques are limited to students 13 years old or older. Although chocking techniques are illustrated in this booklet, the knowledge of how to do it must be taught by your Sensei

Now, you are going to learn chocking techniques. These are a few particular and delicate techniques. You don't apply choking quick and hard. You only study these techniques under the supervision of your sensei

You must release right away when your partner taps

When you feel the choke working and you want to give up, you must tap with you hand on yourself or on your partner more than twice. You can also use your foot to tap the mat.

HADAKA JIME (NAKED OR BARE HANDED CHOKE)

Keep your right knee up and touching the uke's back. Your left knee is on the mat and you must keep your left toes on the mat. Bring your right arm on top of his shoulder and place your right thumb knuckle against the uke's neck.

Grasp both of your hands together and stop the uke from moving his head by locking it into place with the force from your head. Lean the uke backward in order to tighten the grip.

Hey!! Take it easy... Easy... easy...

Defense against Hadaka Jime
Hold tori's right wrist with your left hand and hold his right elbow with your right hand and pull his right arm away from your neck. Turning you head to the right is also important.

When uke gives up by tapping, stop your choke.

I'm sorry Sensei.

Hadaka jime- Choking with your bare hands.

OKURI ERI JIME *(SLIDING COLLAR CHOKE)*

Keep your right knee up and touching your uke's back. Keep your left knee on the mat and your left toes also on the mat. Insert your left arm under the uke's left armpit and grasp their left lapel with your left hand, then pull it downward. Bring your right arm to the top of your partners shoulder and grasp their left upper collar with your right hand while placing your right thumb/wrist again the uke's neck. Then move your left hand to the uke's right lapel and start choking with your right wrist at the same time pulling their right lapel downward. Make the uke off balanced slightly backward and keep your right cheek against the uke's left cheek.

DEFENSE AGAINST OKURI ERI JIME

Grab tori's right sleeve around the elbow area with both of your hands. Turn your face to the right (towards the choking arm) and pull your chin in tight and make a space. Once you have created a space between his right arm and your chin, start to lift your partner's right arm upward with your hands to escape.

KATA HA JIME (ONE-SIDED SHOULDER CHOKE)

Similar to okuri eri jime. Open uke's left lapel with your left hand. Then catch uke's left collar deep with your thumb under the collar, pull down.

Your left arm comes under uke's left arm, first pushing it out, and then driving your left hand behind uke's head. Pull backward and turn right to choke.

RYOTE JIME (TWO HANDED CHOKE)

I grab my uke's lapel with both my hands and go down as if applying a tomoe nage. I start squeezing the ukes neck with my hands.

You must release your choke when your partner taps.

KATA JUJI JIME (HALF CROSS-HANDED CHOKE)

This choke is done by grabbing your opponent's collar with your hands crossed, like this. My left palm up and my right palm facing downward.

Once I straddle the uke, grab his right collar with my right hand and pull it up. Then I slide my left hand inside of the uke's right collar and grab it. The thumb side of my wrist is contacting my uke's neck.

I then grab his left collar with my right hand, thumb inside of his collar. I cover his body with my chest at the same time start choking with my left hand while pulling and pushing with my right hand around his larynx area.

DEFENSE AGAINST KATA JUJI JIME
Place your hand on the tori's elbows and push them upwards and towards each other. Also you can block the choke by sliding your hand under uke's choking hand while placing your palm against your face.

Note:
Nami Juji - Both palms down
Gyaku Juji - Both palms up.

ASHI GATAME JIME (LEG LOCK CHOKE)

From yoko shiho gatame reach across the uke, trapping his left arm with your right arm grabbing his lapel. Your right hand grabs the back of his collar deeply.

Start the choke by stepping over his head with your left leg. Tighten the choke by sliding your head forward into the mat.

SODE GURUMA JIME (SLEEVE-WHEEL CHOKE)

See YouTube USJA - *Choke Escapes*
www.youtube.com/watch?v=01m9KmSq0al

BLOCKING & ESCAPES FROM CHOKES

In choking the opponent usually places his arm under your jaw pressing the side of his hand or wrist against the side of your neck. This squeezes against the large artery on the side of your neck stopping the blood flow to the brain. Your first action is to prevent being choked. Imitate a turtle by lifting your shoulders making your neck disappear into your body. This will cause your opponents arm to end up across your jaw, which is not legal. Another way of blocking chokes is to cross your arms under your jaw and against your neck.

   - If the opponent is able to get a barehanded choke on you, then reach up with both hands grabbing the opponent's wrist and forearm. Now pull down hard twisting his wrist and forearm, pushing the arm away and turning your head in toward your body.

   - If the opponent uses a sliding collar type choke, reach up with both arms catching his sleeve above the elbow of the choking arm. Now pull down hard then snap your hands forward pushing his elbow away as you turn inwards and towards him to escape.

   - If the opponent uses a cross type choke, slide your hand under his choking arm and place the palm of your hand against your face. At this point he will actually be choking against your arm which will stop the choke.

KANSETSU WAZA

(JOINT LOCKS)

Now you will learn the joint lock techniques (Kansetsu waza). Kansetsu waza are directed against the opponents joints, which are twisted, stretched or bent with hands, arms, or legs.

UDE GATAME (STRAIGHT ARM LOCK)

First method: As I approach the uke from his right side, uke reaches for you with his left arm. Quickly place the palm of my closed right hand or my forearm, or slightly above the back of his elbow and press it down until his left wrist meets my right shoulder and his arms is straight. Clasp my left hand over my right, and while controlling his body with my legs and twisting to my right, press down on his elbow with both hands.

Defense
Instead of attempting to pull
your arm free, push it past your
opponent's shoulder to bend it.

NOTE:
You can receive a hansoku maki
if you are not the right age to be attempting
this move!

UDE GARAMI (ENTANGLED ARM LOCK)

First method: As I approach my uke's right side, she raises her left hand and attempts to grab my lapel. I grab the inner side of her left wrist with my left hand, the back of my hand leans over her and presses her arm down, outside her left shoulder. The elbow should be bent. I then slip my right hand under her left upper arm and clasp my left wrist. While holding her wrist I apply pressure on her elbow by using my right forearm as a lever against the back of her upper arm.

Defense

To defend against the first method, grab your own left wrist with your right hand and turn your body to the left and stand up.

Against the second method, raise your upper body, grab your own belt or jacket with your left hand and roll over to your left. If the attacker then tries to apply the technique from behind, stand before they can get their hands in place.

Second Method: Lean over uke from her right side, take her left wrist in my right hand, and bend her arm until it forms a right angle. Reach under her upper arm with my left hand and grab my right wrist. While raising my shoulders I press her wrist down with my right hand and force her left elbow up with my left forearm.

HIZA GATAME (KNEE ARM LOCK)

As uke grips my left lapel with his right hand I quickly trap it in my right armpit and grab his right lapel with my left hand. I then put my left foot against the upper part or his right thigh or groin and push, thereby breaking his balance forward. Control him by bending your right leg and putting your foot a little above the left side of his belt. At the same time, twist my hips to my left, place the inner side of my knee on the outside of his elbow, and press down hard.

DEFENSE

1. Twist your right wrist clockwise and pull it out of your opponent's armpit.
2. Push your arm through his armpit to relive the pressure on the elbow.
3. Roll forward over his body

164

JUJI GATAME (CROSS ARM LOCK)

I am kneeling on my left knee to the right side of the uke. Uke reaches up for my lapel with his right arm. Take his arm in my hands, placing both my palms on the inner side, my thumbs on the outside. Pull with both hands and place the front of my right shin up against his right side, then roll backward, dropping my hips as close to his shoulder as possible and placing my left leg over his throat and chest so his can't sit up. While holding the arm with the inner side up, lift my hips and pull down on his wrist with both hands.

DEFENSE

1. With your left hand grab your right wrist or lower right sleeve before the opponent can take hold of it. Then twist/bend to your right.

2. If caught in this lock turn, bend your arm until your elbow points to the side. Push your attacker's leg away with your left hand and roll your body to the left until it is parallel with your attackers, then pull your arms free.

WAKI GATAME (ARMPIT ARM LOCK)

I grip the uke's left wrist from uke's left side with my left hand then right hand. Pull his left arm towards me and place it under my armpit. Stretch his elbow and lock the straightened arm.

NOTE: Hansoku penalty can be given if armlock is applied by dropping against arm

HARA GATAME (STOMACH ARM LOCK)

I grip uke's left wrist from the uke's left side
with my left hand. Then I place my stomach against his
left elbow, at the same time, I reach his left lapel with my right hand and
grab it. I start applying pressure to his elbow and lock the elbow straight,
while applying the choke with my right hand to keep his body
from moving forward and prevent
him from standing.

See YouTube USJA - *Armlock Escapes*

www.youtube.com/watch?v=KcF0UyiZXQ8

BLOCKING & ESCAPES FROM ARMLOCKS

In order to initiate an arm lock, the opponent will either grab your wrist or will hook your arm. Therefore, to stop an arm lock you must always keep your elbows close to your side and turn in towards the attacker. Also, as a defensive move you can cross your arms alongside your neck pressing your elbows against your body. In order to stop the opponent from wrenching back on your arm you can cross your other arm over the attacked arm and press it against your chest.

In the case of a cross armlock (juji-gatame) you escape by changing directions, (1) quickly turning towards opponent while pulling your elbow into your side, (2) swinging your legs up and over your shoulder and (3) rolling on your stomach while bringing your legs towards his feet.

NAGE-NO-KATA

Katas are prearranged forms of techniques in which each move is precisely described. Nage-no-Kata was the first Kata that Shihan Kano developed for judo. Since one of Kano's objectives was to develop a well-rounded person, both physically and mentally, he selected a series of throwing techniques that in total utilized all of one's muscles. Each of the techniques are practiced on both the right and left side. In this kata the thrower is called "Tori" and the receiver is called "Uke." Both players synchronize moves in a smooth continuous manner. The Uke's function is especially important because he usually initiates the attack. This kata includes 15 throwing techniques broken into five groups of three techniques each as follows:

Te-waza (Hand Techniques)
(1) Uki-otoshi, (2) Seoi-nage, (3) Kata-guruma

Koshi-waza (Hip-Techniques)
(1) Uki-goshi, (2) Harai-goshi, (3) Tsurikomi-goshi

Ashi-waza (Leg Techniques)
(1) Okuri-ashi-harai, (2) Sasae-tsurikomi-ashi, (3) Uchi-mata

Ma-sutemi-waza (Rear Sacrifice Techniques)
(1) Tomoe-nage, (2) Ura-nage, (3) Sumi-gaeshi

Yoko-sutemi-waza (Side Sacrifice Techniques)
(1) Yoko-gake, (2) Yoko-guruma, (3) Uki-waza

Also see, YouTube USJA - *Nage-no-Kata*

www.youtube.com/watch?v=MGk16rYVEog

For a detail description of Nage-no-Kata. Read *"Judo Formal Techniques"* by Otaki and Draeger.

UKI OTOSHI

KATA GURUMA

SEOI NAGE

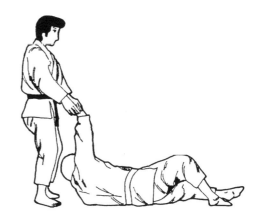

KOSHI-WAZA

UKE GOSHI

HARAI-GOSHI

TSURIKOMI-GOSHI

ASHI-WAZA

OKURI-ASHI-HARAI

SASAE-TSURIKOMI-ASHI

UCHI MATA

MA-SUTEMI-WAZA

TOMOE-NAGE

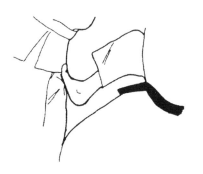

URA-NAGE

SUMI-GAESHI

 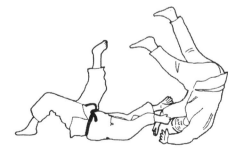

YOKO-SUTEMI-WAZA

UKI-WAZA

YOKO-GURUMA

YOKO-GAKE

SELF-DEFENSE

So you want to go zip and throw the big bully with a magic trick. You can. It will look like magic but is not so simple. The physical movement is easy enough, but the big problem is not your opponent, but your own self-control. In a fight you are scared and you may feel a little weak. The scared feeling you have is healthy and normal, fear stimulates you, makes you faster and stronger. What you need is mental and physical confidence. Training in sport judo will give you this through exercises, tumbling, free practice, games and tournaments. In free practice and tournaments you learn to work under pressure and to apply your techniques in the most efficient manner. Sport judo techniques are some of the strongest and most skillful

self-defense techniques because you learn to have complete control of your opponent at all times.

Many people come to the judo school saying they only want to learn self-defense and not sport judo. The difference between the two is the method of training as it is in all self-defense. If you only practice self-defense tricks you are fooling yourself for you will be limited to defense against a cooperating opponent. You must practice under realistic conditions if you are to become skillful with confidence.

Fighting is a serious business, there is no halfway about it. The most skillful fighter will try to avoid a fight and leave as friends with his once enemy.

LEGAL LIMITS ON SELF-DEFENSE

We cannot give you legal advice, however, the following are general guidelines regarding the use of self-defense. The laws on self-defense vary from state to state, but in general you are allowed to use reasonable physical force to protect yourself from imminent or immediate physical injury. You can only use that amount of force that's necessary to stop the threat of harm. Most states have special rules for the use of deadly force. Again, the rules vary by state, but in general you can't use deadly force unless you're in reasonable fear of immediate serious physical injury or death. In most states you have the duty to retreat before using deadly force. In other words, deadly force needs to be the last and only resort. If you can escape from the situation safely, you have a duty to do so. If you can escape and don't, and then use deadly force, you could be charged with a crime.

A useful defense when threatened or bullied is a loud scream, so practice screaming loud in your self-defense class. Most attackers or bullies prey on the weak and they themselves are cowards and can be easily embarrassed or deterred by your scream.

Another useful tool to avoid conflict is the use of verbal judo, such as:

"My judo teacher says I should not use judo because I might break your bones or skull."

"My uncle is a cop who will take care of you."

"The principal or my parents will talk to your folks"

"I am really sick and don't want you to catch what I have."

If you cannot prevent a fight, next try to avoid a person's movement and take him down trying not to injure him. But if all fails, you must fight hard, throwing, striking or whatever is necessary to defeat your opponent quickly. Remember that when someone tries to injure you, he is mentally disturbed and off balance. If you remain calm and do not show your feelings, he will not be sure of himself and possibly call it off. Watch the general area of his head and shoulders so that when he moves you will naturally avoid or block. Your defense is really an attack at the right moment, so move fast and hard.

In this manual we have chosen not to discuss punching, kicking or the use of weapons for self-defense purposes. This is a complex subject which has to be tailored to the attendees in any self-defense class. If you are a student of martial arts it is natural and easier to use the techniques you have practiced in your art, such as judo, karate, boxing, etc. Again remember there are legal limits on self-defense so it is better to avoid injuring the attacker or bullied if possible.

Rather than illustrate self-defense techniques we have provided you with three YouTube videos. The first video shows techniques that we use in USJA's promotion system applying straight judo techniques, without gripping the judo-gi, for self-defense. This was demonstrated by the students at Discover Judo Club. Although these are not considered "deadly techniques", they can be harmful to an opponent, so try to avoid injury. "Deadly arts" are unnecessary except in warfare or life-threatening situations, and then you must be a little crazy to use them. As calmness and a clear mind is your strength, to think of "deadly arts" will only weaken you. Knights and samurai were gentlemen, not nice guys, because it was a necessity of warfare to be in control of your mind.

The second self-defense YouTube video shows the use of various judo related techniques by sensei Tsukamoto.

The third self-defense YouTube video shows the use of judo – aikido related techniques developed by sensei Tomiki for use by judoka. Techniques shown in this video are by Aikido Shihan Satoh, a professor from Waseda University, Tokyo.

SEE THE FOLLOWING VIDEOS:

YouTube USJA - *Self-defense Discover Judo*

www.youtube.com/watch?v=ZGac3PJwRoU

YouTube USJA - *Self-defense Tsukamoto*

www.youtube.com/watch?v=y8GdYCpuQIM

YouTube USJA - *Self-defense Satoh*

www.youtube.com/watch?v=v5D8PP15a0E

GUIDE TO TOURNAMENT

KNOWING THE RULES

Most tournaments are based on the International Judo Federation (IJF) rules. Rules and interpretations change and a tournament may have exceptions to the rules. For this guide we used the published IJF rules as of October 2013. This guideline attempts to simplify the rules so that the player knows how to win and how not to lose by violating a rule.

THE MAT AREA

The contest area is usually between 24 to 30 ft. square, surrounded by a safety zone of about 9 to 12 feet. The dynamic edge rule allows you to continue fighting and score outside of the contest area as long as your action started within the contest area. If the player steps outside or pushes his opponent outside the contest area, not due to an attacking action, the player may receive a Shido penalty.

MATCH TIME

Normally, time for juniors may run from 2.5 to 5 minutes. Golden Score, which is an overtime situation, does not have a time limit. Since there may be several contests going on at the same time you may be confused by signals or commands from other mats. Do not stop fighting unless you get a direct command from your referee.

WHITE OR BLUE DESIGNATIONS

Before a player enters a contest area to fight, he will be designated as white or blue. At national or international tournaments players are required to have both a white and blue judo-gi. At the local and regional tournaments players may be required to only wear the white judo-gi, and provide their own white and blue belt. At these tournaments blue judo-gi may be optional however, if the player is designated as white, then he must have a white judo-gi.

JUDO-GI

The size of the player's judo-gi is an important matter. If the player enters the mat and has an improper judo-gi the penalty will be a Hansoku-make, a loss. Judo-gi sizing must be checked before entering the mat. The main dimensions for the jacket and pants are that the sleeve shall cover the wrist

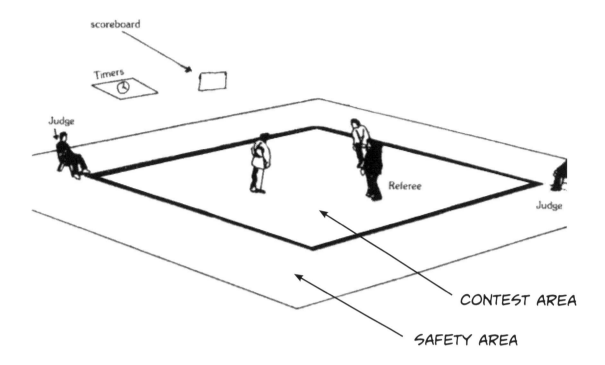

and that the pants are not more than 2 inches above the ankle bone . The belt should not be more than 8 inches below the knot. Judo-gi needs to be clean. The IJF rules contain more information on judo-gi sizing including limitations on patches. Men are not allowed to wear clothing under their jackets. There are special rules for women as follows;

Female contestant's shall wear under the jacket either 1) A plain white or off-white T-shirt, with short sleeves, rather strong, long enough to be worn inside the trousers, or 2) A plain white or off-white leotard with short sleeves.

HYGIENE

THE IJF RULES STATE
(a) The Judogi shall be clean, generally dry and without unpleasant odor.
(b) The nails of the feet and hands shall be cut short.
(c) The personal hygiene of the contestant shall be of a high standard.
(d) Long hair shall be tied so as to avoid causing inconvenience to the other contestant

HOW WINS ARE SCORED

An Ippon score is an automatic win. Two Waza-ari scores equal an Ippon. If there is no Ippon score when the match time expires, then the win will be based on the highest score obtained, such as, waza-ari, yuko or penalty by opponent. If the score is even at the end of the match, there will not be a decision, and the players will go into overtime called "Golden Score." During this time a win is awarded to the first player to score, or if his opponent receives a penalty.

SCORING BY THROW

An Ippon is scored if the opponent is thrown with control, force and speed, and lands mostly on his back. In other words you have to really slam your opponent. If the throw seems to lack any of the elements then the referee may call it a Waza-ari. In other words a slow throw,i.e. Tomoe-nage, is not an Ippon throw. If a player scores a Waza-ari, then the second Waza-ari scored will be declared Waza-ari-awasete- ippon. If the opponent is thrown on his side then a Yuko is given. Yuko scores are not accumulated, however, if neither player receives Waza-ari or each has scored a Waza-ari, then the one with the most Yuko scores wins. If neither player has a score than the one with the least amount of Shido penalties would win.

SCORING BY KATAME-WAZA

When you obtain a hold the referee will start the count by calling out Osaekomi . The IJF defines holding as , "The contestant being held must be controlled by his opponent and must have his back, both shoulders or one shoulder in contact with the Tatami." Holding time scores Ippon (20 seconds), Waza-ari (15 seconds) and Yuko (10 seconds). Your body needs to be in either Kesa (sitting sideways, legs split apart) , Shiho (stomach down and legs apart) position or Ura-gatame. If your opponent starts to break the hold and you shift to another hold, time will continue to count. If opponent turns to his stomach, sits up or scissors one of your legs, the referee will stop the time by calling out Toketa. However, players may continue to fight. During Osaekomi, if the referee wants to freeze the action (stop in place) for awarding a penalty or for any other reason, he will place his hand on the top player and call the command Sono-mama. The players will freeze in place. To restart fighting, the referee will call Yoshi. If the referee wants to break up the mat work he will call Mate and the players will return to a standing position.

Strangling or choking (Shime-waza) opponent is only allowed for players 13 and over. You cannot choke with your fingers or the end of the judo-gi or belt. You cannot put your hand on opponent's face in trying to choke. Ippon is scored if the opponent taps out at least twice or passes out.

Armlocks are not allowed for players under black belt. Brown belts may sign waivers. There is no age limit if the person fights as a brown or black belt. In international competition "Junior Cadets" may use armlocks. Ippon is scored if the player taps out twice or is injured.

PENALTIES

There are two groups of penalties (1) *Shido* , for slight infringements and (2) *Hansoku-make* for grave infringements. There are over 30 specific penalties listed in the IJF rules. The reasons for these penalties are for safety, negative or defensive judo, specifically prohibited acts and actions that may be against the spirit of judo. Shido penalties do not convert to Yuko or Waza-ari rewards for the other player. However, 4 shidos penalize the player with a Hansoku-make loss, thereby giving his opponent an Ippon win. A summary of penalties is as follows;

SHIDO - Immediate penalty

Breaking grip with two hands; cover edge of judo jacket to prevent grip; does not engage in quick gripping; continually breaks opponent's grip; grips opponent's wrist or hands to avoid being gripped; false attack (without intent of throwing); without gripping or releases grip, or does not break opponents balance; circle the end of the belt jacket around any part of opponent; take your opponent's judo-gi in your mouth; put hand, arm, foot or leg directly in opponent's face; put foot or leg in opponent's belt; collar or lapel; apply choking using bottom of jacket or belt or only with fingers; leg scissor opponent's trunk, neck or head; kick with knee or foot opponent's hand or arm to break grip; bend opponent's fingers back; excessive defensive posture; interlock or hold opponent's fingers with one or two hands; or pushing opponent out of contest area.

SHIDO - After failing to attack immediately

When cross gripping jacket or gripping the belt or side; pistol or pocket grip on the bottom of the sleeve; force opponent to take bending position; when stepping out of the contest area.

SHIDO - approximately 25 seconds.

Not to make any attacking moves.

HANSOKU-MAKE - player is expelled from tournament.

Apply Kawazu-gake; apply Kansetsu-waza other than to elbow joint; lift and drive opponent's back into mat; reap supporting leg from inside; disregard referee's instructions; make unnecessary calls, remarks or gestures to opponent or referee; action that may endanger or injure opponent's neck or spine or against spirit of judo; fall directly to mat by applying a technique such as Waki-gatame ; intentionally fall on back when opponent is clinging to you.

HANSOKU-MAKE - penalty only applies to immediate contest.

After three(3) Shidos, a fourth is committed; head dive into mat; wear hard or metallic object; enter mat with illegal judo-gi; in Tachiwaza ,attack or touch opponent below the belt.

Referee hand signals as shown on the next page.

TIPS

As you can see there are numerous and confusing ways to lose by penalty. In competition it is natural to be nervous and grip tightly thereby letting your opponent anticipate your move and block your actions. This could be penalized as a "false attack". Also, it is natural to try to avoid your opponent's throws making you appear to be defensive and be penalized. What experienced competitors do is to have a positive attitude and not appear to be defending. In order to break an opponent's balance you must obtain a strong grip with your pulling arm that will control the opponents elbow or shoulder. Attack at the moment your opponent is most vulnerable. It is easier to throw one who is moving because they are on one leg than when they stand upright with both legs on the ground. See the section on"Chance".

Judo Referee's Hand Signals

Referee: Signaling an Ippon Score *Ippon*	
Referee: Indicating Wazari Score *Wazari*	
Referee: Indicating a Yuko Score *Yuko*	
Wazari awasete Ippon: Judoka has one wazari and then scores another wazari. The referee will announce *Wazari awasete Ippon*	
Nullifying a previous score *Nullifying Score*	
Referee: Signaling Matte (Break) *Mate*	
Referee: Indicating the start of Osaekomi (pin) *Start of Osaekomi*	
Referee: Indicating "Toketa" . The osaekomi (pin) is nullified. *Toketa*	

Judo Referee's Hand Signals

Referee: Indicating mate (break) in newaza (matwork) *Mate in Newaza*	
Side judge: Indicating that the action was inbounds *In bounds*	
Side Judge: Indicating action was "out of bounds" *Out of bounds*	
Side Judge: Nullifying a score/action *Nullifying a Score*	
Referee: indicating non-combativity (stalling) *Non-combativity*	
Referee indicating to the judoka to fix his/her judogi. *Fix Judogi*	
Referee: Indicating he wants both judoka's to stop moving *Sonomama!*	
Referee: Indicating "Yoshi" for both contestants to begin action. *Yoshi*	

GENERAL TERMINOLOGY - ENGLISH TO JAPANESE

DOJO USAGE

ATTENTION	KIYOTSUKE
BALANCE BREAKING	KUZUSHI
BELT	OBI
BODY MOVEMENT	TAI-SABAKI
BREAK-FALLING	UKEMI
CONCENTRATION OF SPIRIT	KIAI
CONTEST	SHIAI
EFFECTIVE PREFERRED TECHNIQUE	TOKUI-WAZA
EXECUTOR OF A TECHNIQUE	TORI
FIRST DEGREE BLACK BELT (FIRST-STEP)	SHODAN
FORM PRACTICE	KATA
FORMAL SITTING	SEIZA
FREE PRACTICE	RANDORI
GENTLE ART	JU-JITSU
GENTLE WAY	JUDO
INFORMAL SITTING CROSS LEGGED	ANZA
JUDO PRACTITIONER	JUDOKA
JUDO UNIFORM	JUDOGI
KNEELING SALUTATION	ZAREI
LEFT	HIDARI
LEVEL OF BLACK BELT RANK	DAN
MATTING	TATAMI
MAX. EFFICIENCY WITH MIN. EFFORT	SEIRYOKU-ZENYO
MUTUAL WELFARE AND BENEFIT	KITA-KYOE
POSITIONING OR ENTRY	TSUKURI
PRACTICE HALL	DOJO
RECEIVER OF A TECHNIQUE	UKE
REPETITION TRAINING	UCHIKOMI
RIGHT	MIGI
SALUTATION	REI
SANDAL (JAPANESE STYLE)	ZORI
STANDING SALUTATION	RITSUREI
TEACHER	SENSEI
TECHNIQUE	WAZA
THE FOUNDING SCHOOL OF JUDO	KODOKAN
THROWING ACTION	KAKE
UPPER PLACE OR SIDE OF DOJO	JOSEKI

COMPETITION TERMINOLOGY

BEGIN!	HAJIME!
COMPLETE POINT	IPPON
CONTINUE	YOSHI
DECISION	HANTEI
DISQUALIFICATION	HANSOKU-MAKE
DO NOT MOVE!	SONO-MAMA!
DRAW	HIKIWAKI
HOLD BROKEN!	TOKETA!
HOLDING	OSAEKOMI
NEAR IPPON SCORE	WAZA-ARI
SECOND WAZA-ARI	WAZA-ARI/AWASETE IPPON

SMALL INFRINGEMENT . . . . SHIDO
SMALL SCORE. . . . . YUKO
THAT IS ALL! . . . . SORE-MADE!
WAIT!. . . . . MATE!

TECHNIQUE TERMINOLOGY

HAND TECHNIQUES . . . . TE-WAZA
BELT DROP. . . . . OBI-OTOSHI
BODY DROP . . . . TAI-OTOSHI
CORNER DROP . . . . SUMI-OTOSHI
DEAD TREE DROP. . . . . KUCHIKI-TAOSHI
FLOATING DROP. . . . . UKI-OTOSHI
HEEL TRIP REVERSAL . . . . KIBISU-GAESHI
INNER THIGH REAPING THROW SLIP . . . . UCHIMATA-SUKASHI
MINOR INNER REAPING REVERSAL. . . . . KOUCHI-GAESHI
MOUNTAIN STORM . . . . YAMA-ARASHI
ONE-ARMED SHOULDER THROW . . . . IPPON-SEOI-NAGE
SCOOPING THROW. . . . . SUKUI-NAGE
SHOULDER DROP . . . . SEOI-OTOSHI
SHOULDER WHEEL . . . . KATA-GURUMA
TWO-ARMED SHOULDER THROW . . . . MOROTE-SEOI-NAGE
TWO HANDED REAP. . . . . MOROTE-GARI

HIP TECHNIQUES   KOSHI-WAZA

BACK HIP THROW . . . . USHIRO-GOSHI
FLOATING HIP THROW . . . . UKI-GOSHI
HIGH LIFT . . . . DAKI-AGE
HIP WHEEL . . . . KOSHI-GURUMA
LIFTING HIP THROW . . . . TSURI-GOSHI
LIFT PULL HIP THROW . . . . TSURIKOMI-GOSHI
MAJOR HIP THROW. . . . . O-GOSHI
SLEEVE LIFT PULL HIP THROW . . . . SODE-TSURIKOMI-GOSHI
SPRINGING HIP THROW . . . . HANE-GOSHI
SWEEPING HIP THROW . . . . HARAI-GOSHI
SWITCHING HIP THROW . . . . UTSURI-GOSHI

FOOT/LEG TECHNIQUES   ASHI-WAZA

ADVANCING FOOT SWEEP . . . . DEASHI-HARAI
HEEL TRIP. . . . . KIBUSU-GAESHI
INNER THIGH REAPING THROW COUNTER . . . . UCHIMATA-GAESHI
INNER THIGH REAPING THROW . . . . UCHIMATA
KNEE WHEEL. . . . . HIZA-GURUMA
LEG WHEEL . . . . ASHI-GURUMA
MAJOR INNER REAPING. . . . . O-UCHI-GARI
MAJOR INNER REAPING COUNTER. O-UCHI-GAESHI
MAJOR OUTER DROP . . . . O-SOTO-OTOSHI
MAJOR OUTER REAPING . . . . O-SOTO-GARI
MAJOR OUTER REAPING COUNTER . . . . O-SOTO-GAESHI
MAJOR OUTER WHEEL . . . . O-SOTO-GURUMA
MAJOR WHEEL . . . . O-GURUMA
MINOR INNER REAPING . . . . KOUCHI-GARI
MINOR OUTER HOOK . . . . KOSOTO-GAKE

MINOR OUTER REAPING. . . . . KOSOTO-GARI
PROPPING DRAWING ANKLE THROW . . . . SASAE-TSURIKOMI-ASHI
SPRING HIP COUNTER THROW . . . . HANE-GOSHI-GAESHI
SWALLOW COUNTER . . . . TSUBAME-GAESHI
SWEEPING ANKLE THROW . . . . OKURI-ASHI-HARAI
SWEEPING DRAWING ANKLE THROW. . . . . HARAI-TSURIKOMI-ASHI
SWEEPING HIP THROW COUNTER. . . . . HARAI-GOSHI-GAESHI

REAR SACRIFICE TECHNIQUES   MA-SUTEMI-WAZA

CIRCLE THROW (STOMACH THROW). . . . . TOMOE-NAGE
CORNER THROW . . . . SUMI-GAESHI
PULLING DOWN SACRIFICE THROW. . . . . HIKKOMI-GAESHI
REAR THROW . . . . URA-NAGE
RICE BALE THROW . . . . TAWARA-GAESHI

SIDE SACRIFICE TECHNIQUES   YOKO-SUTEMI-WAZA

FLOATING THROW . . . . UKI-WAZA
INNER THIGH WRAP-AROUND THROW . . . . UCHIMATA-MAKIKOMI
INNER WINDING THROW . . . . UCHI-MAKIKOMI
MAJOR OUTSIDE WRAP AROUND THROW. . . . . O-SOTO-MAKIKOMI
OUTER WRAP AROUND THROW . . . . SOTO-MAKIKOMI
REAR TRUNK SEPARATION . . . . DAKI-WAKARE
SCISSORS THROW. . . . . KANI-BASAMI (FORBIDDEN)
SIDE BODY DROP . . . . YOKO-GAKE
SIDE CIRCLE THROW . . . . YOKO-TOMOE-NAGE
SIDE DROP . . . . YOKO-OTOSHI
SIDE SEPARATION . . . . YOKO-WAKARE
SIDE WHEEL . . . . YOKO-GURUMA
SINGLE LEG ENTANGLEMENT . . . . KAWAZU-GAKE (FORBIDDEN)
SMALL INNER WRAP AROUND THROW. . . . . KOUCHI-MAKIKOMI
SPRINGING WRAP AROUND THROW . . . . HANE-MAKIKOMI
SWEEPING HIP WRAP-AROUND THROW . . . . HARAI-MAKIKOMI
VALLEY DROP . . . . TANI-OTOSHI

HOLD DOWN TECHNIQUES   OSAEKOMI-WAZA

FLOATING HOLD. . . . . UKI-GATAME
MODIFIED SCARF HOLD. . . . . KUZURE-KESA-GATAME
MODIFIED UPPER FOUR CORNERS HOLD. . . . . KUZURE-KAMISHIHO-GATAME
MODIFIED SIDE FOUR CORNERS HOLD . . . . KUZURE-YOKO-SHIHO-GATAME
MODIFIED STRAIGHT FOUR CORNERS HOLD . . . . KUZURE-TATE-SHIHO-GATAME
SCARF HOLD. . . . . KESA-GATAME
SHOULDER HOLD. . . . . KATA-GATAME
SIDE FOUR CORNERS HOLD . . . . YOKO-SHIHO-GATAME
STRAIGHT FOUR CORNERS HOLD. . . . . TATE-SHIHO-GATAME
UPPER FOUR CORNERS HOLD . . . . KAMI-SHIHO-GATAME
REVERSE SCARF HOLD . . . . USHIRO-KESA-GATAME

STRANGLING TECHNIQUES   SHIME-WAZA

BODY SCISSORS; TRUNK STRANGLE. . . . . DOJIME (FORBIDDEN)
HALF CROSS STRANGLE. . . . . KATA-JUJI-JIME
NAKED STRANGLE . . . . HADAKA-JIME
NORMAL CROSS STRANGLE . . . . NAMI-JUJI-JIME

ONE HAND STRANGLE . . . . KATA-TE-JIME
REVERSE CROSS STRANGLE . . . . GYAKU-JUJI-JIME
SINGLE WING STRANGLE. . . . . KATAHA-JIME
SLEEVE WHEEL STRANGLE. . . . . SODE-GURUMA-JIME
SLIDING COLLAR STRANGLE . . . . OKURI-ERI-JIME
THRUSTING STRANGLE. . . . . TSUKKOMI-JIME
TRIANGULAR STRANGLE . . . . SANKAKU-JIME
TWO HANDED CHOKE . . . . RYOTE-JIME

JOINT-LOCK TECHNIQUES   KANSETSU-WAZA

ARMPIT ARMLOCK . . . . WAKI-GATAME
CROSS ARMLOCK . . . . JUJI-GATAME
ENTANGLED ARMLOCK . . . . UDE-GARAMI
HAND ARMLOCK . . . . TE-GATAME
KNEE ARMLOCK . . . . HIZA-GATAME
LEG ARMLOCK. . . . . ASHI-GATAME
LEG ENTANGLEMENT . . . . ASHI-GARAMI (FORBIDDEN)
REVERSE ENTANGLED ARMLOCK . . . . GYAKU-UDE-GARAMI
STOMACH ARMLOCK . . . . HARA-GATAME
STRAIGHT ARM ARMLOCK. . . . . UDE-GATAME
TRIANGULAR ARMLOCK . . . . SANKAKU-GATAME

BREAK-FALLS   UKEMI

FORWARD ROLLING BREAK-FALL . . . . ZEMPO-KAITEN-UKEMI
FRONT BREAK-FALL. . . . . MAE-UKEMI
REAR BREAK-FALL. . . . . USHIRO-UKEMI
SIDE BREAK-FALL . . . . YOKO-UKEMI

FORMAL EXERCISES   KATA

FORMS OF ANTIQUE . . . . KOSHIKI-NO-KATA
FORMS OF DECISION. . . . . KIME-NO-KATA
FORMS OF FIVE. . . . . ITSUTSU-NO-KATA
FORMS OF GENTLENESS . . . . JUNO-KATA
FORMS OF GRAPPLING. . . . . KATAME-NO-KATA
FORMS OF SELF-DEFENSE . . . . GOSHINJITSU
FORMS OF THROWING . . . . NAGE-NO-KATA

MISCELLANEOUS

ALL GRAPPLING TECHNIQUES . . . . KATAME-WAZA
COMBINATION TECHNIQUES . . . . RENRAKU-WAZA
CONTINUOUS COMBINATION OF TECHNIQUES . . . . RENZOKU-WAZA
COUNTER TECHNIQUES . . . . KAESHI-WAZA
GRAPPLING TECHNIQUES (NON STANDING) . . . . NEWAZA
STRIKING TECHNIQUES. . . . . ATEMI-WAZA
THROWING FORMS. . . . . NAGE-NO-KATA
THROWING TECHNIQUES . . . . NAGE-WAZA
THROWS EXECUTED WHILE STANDING . . . . TACHI-WAZA

GENERAL TERMINOLOGY – JAPANESE TO ENGLISH

DOJO USAGE

ANZA . . . . INFORMAL SITTING CROSS LEGGED
DAN . . . . LEVEL OF BLACK BELT RANK
DOJO . . . . PRACTICE HALL
HIDARI . . . . LEFT
JOSEKI . . . . UPPER PLACE OR SIDE OF DOJO
JUDO . . . . GENTLE WAY (GIVING WAY)
JUDOGI . . . . JUDO UNIFORM
JUDOKA . . . . JUDO PRACTITIONER
JUJITSU . . . . GENTLE ART
KAKE . . . . THROWING ACTION
KATA . . . . FORM PRACTICE
KIAI . . . . CONCENTRATION OF SPIRIT
JITA KYOEI . . . . MUTUAL WELFARE AND BENEFIT
KIOTSUKE . . . . ATTENTION!
KODOKAN . . . . THE FOUNDING SCHOOL OF JUDO
KUZUSHI . . . . BALANCE BREAKING
MIGI . . . . RIGHT
OBI . . . . BELT
RANDORI . . . . FREE PRACTICE
REI . . . . BOW
RITSUREI . . . . STANDING BOW
SEIRYOKU ZENYO . . . . MAXIMUM EFFICIENCY
. . . . WITH MINIMUM EFFORT
SEIZA . . . . FORMAL SITTING
SENSEI . . . . TEACHER
SHIAI . . . . CONTEST
SHODAN . . . . FIRST DEGREE BLACK BELT (FIRST STEP)
TAI-SABAKI . . . . BODY MOVEMENT
TATAMI . . . . JAPANESE FLOORING MAT
TOKUI-WAZA . . . . EFFECTIVE PREFERRED TECHNIQUE
TORI . . . . EXECUTER OF A TECHNIQUE
TSUKURI . . . . POSITIONING OR ENTRY OF TECHNIQUE
UCHIKOMI . . . . REPETITION TRAINING
UKE . . . . RECEIVER OF A TECHNIQUE
UKEMI . . . . BREAK-FALLING
WAZA . . . . TECHNIQUE
ZAREI . . . . KNEELING BOW
ZORI . . . . SANDAL (JAPANESE STYLE)

COMPETITION TERMINOLOGY

HAJIME! . . . . BEGIN!
HANTEI . . . . DECISION
HIKIWAKE . . . . DRAW
HANSOKU-MAKE . . . . LOSS BY MAJOR INFRACTION
IPPON . . . . COMPLETE POINT
MATE! . . . . WAIT!
OSAEKOMIHOLDING
SHIDO . . . . SMALL INFRINGEMENT
SONO-MAMA! . . . . DO NOT MOVE!
SORE-MADE! . . . . THAT IS ALL!

TOKETA!. . . . . .HOLD BROKEN!

WAZA-ARI . . . . .NEAR IPPON SCORE

WAZA-ARI/AWASETE IPPON . . . . .SECOND WAZA ARI (SCORES IPPON)

YOSHI!. . . . . .CONTINUE!

YUKO . . . . .SMALL SCORE

TECHNIQUE TERMINOLOGY

TE-WAZA. . . . . .HAND TECHNIQUES

IPPON-SEOI-NAGE . . . . .ONE-ARMED SHOULDER THROW

KATA-GURUMA. . . . . .SHOULDER WHEEL

KIBISU-GAESHI . . . . .HEEL TRIP REVERSAL

KOUCHI-GAESHI. . . . . .MINOR INNER REAPING COUNTER

KUCHIKI-TAOSHI. . . . . .DEAD TREE DROP

MOROTE-GARI. . . . . .TWO HANDED REAP

MOROTE-SEOI-NAGE . . . . .TWO-ARMED SHOULDER THROW

OBI-OTOSHI. . . . . .BELT DROP

SEOI-OTOSHI. . . . . .SHOULDER DROP

SUKUI-NAGE . . . . .SCOOPING THROW

SUMI-OTOSHI. . . . . .CORNER DROP

TAI-OTOSHI . . . . .BODY DROP

UCHIMATA-SUKASHI. . . . . .INNER THIGH REAPING THROW SLIP

UKI-OTOSHI. . . . . .FLOATING DROP

YAMA-ARASHI . . . . .MOUNTAIN STORM

KOSHI-WAZA   HIP TECHNIQUES

DAKI-AGE (FORBIDDEN). . . . . .HIGH LIFT

HANE-GOSHI. . . . . .SPRING HIP THROW

HARAI-GOSHI. . . . . .SWEEPING HIP THROW

KOSHI-GURUMA. . . . . .HIP WHEEL

O-GOSHI . . . . .MAJOR HIP THROW

SODE-TSURIKOMI-GOSHI . . . . .SLEEVE LIFT PULL HIP THROW

TSURI-GOSHI . . . . .LIFTING HIP THROW

TSURIKOMI-GOSHI . . . . .LIFT PULL HIP THROW

UKI-GOSHI. . . . . .FLOATING HIP THROW

USHIRO-GOSHI . . . . .BACK HIP THROW

UTSURI-GOSHI. . . . . .SWITCHING HIP THROW

ASHI-WAZA   FOOT/LEG TECHNIQUES

ASHI-GURUMA. . . . . .LEG WHEEL

DEASHI-HARAI. . . . . .ADVANCING FOOT SWEEP

HANE-GOSHI-GAESHI. . . . . .SPRING HIP COUNTER THROW

HARAI-GOSHI-GAESHI . . . . .SWEEPING HIP COUNTER THROW

HARAI-TSURIKOMI-ASHI . . . . .SWEEPING DRAWING ANKLE THROW

HIZA-GURUMA. . . . . .KNEE WHEEL

KIBUSU-GAESHI. . . . . .HEEL TRIP

KOSOTO-GAKE. . . . . .MINOR OUTER HOOK

KOSOTO-GARI. . . . . .MINOR OUTER REAPING

KOUCHI-GARI. . . . . .MINOR INNER REAPING

O-GURUMA . . . . .MAJOR WHEEL

OKURI-ASHI-HARAI. . . . . .SWEEPING ANKLE THROW

O-SOTO-GAESHI . . . . .MAJOR OUTER REAPING COUNTER

O-SOTO-GARI . . . . .MAJOR OUTER REAPING

O-SOTO-GURUMA . . . . MAJOR OUTER WHEEL
O-SOTO-OTOSHI . . . . MAJOR OUTER DROP
O-UCHI-GAESHI . . . . MAJOR INNER REAPING COUNTER
O-UCHI-GARI. . . . . MAJOR INNER REAPING
SASAE-TSURIKOMI-ASHI. . . . . PROPPING DRAWING ANKLE THROW
TSUBAME-GAESHI . . . . SWALLOW COUNTER
UCHIMATA . . . . INNER THIGH REAPING THROW
UCHIMATA-GAESHI. . . . . INNER THIGH REAPING THROW COUNTER

MA-SUTEMI-WAZA   REAR SACRIFICE TECHNIQUES

HIKKOMI-GAESHI . . . . PULLING DOWN SACRIFICE THROW
SUMI-GAESHI . . . . CORNER THROW
TAWARA-GAESHI . . . . RICE BALE THROW
TOMOE-NAGE . . . . CIRCLE THROW (STOMACH THROW)
URA-NAGE. . . . . REAR THROW

YOKO-SUTEMI-WAZA   SIDE SACRIFICE TECHNIQUES

DAKI-WAKARE . . . . REAR TRUNK TURNOVER
HANE-MAKIKOMI . . . . SPRING WRAP-AROUND THROW
HARAI-MAKIKOMI . . . . SWEEPING HIP WRAP-AROUND THROW
KANI-BASAMI(FORBIDDEN). . . . . SCISSORS THROW
KAWAZU-GAKE (FORBIDDEN) . . . . SINGLE LEG ENTANGLEMENT
KOUCHI-MAKIKOMI. . . . . SMALL INNER WRAP AROUND THROW
O-SOTO-MAKIKOMI . . . . MAJOR OUTSIDE WRAP AROUND THROW
SOTO-MAKIKOMI . . . . OUTER WRAP AROUND THROW
TANI-OTOSHI . . . . VALLEY DROP
UCHI-MAKIKOMI. . . . . INNER WINDING THROW
UCHIMATA-MAKIKOMI. . . . . INNER THIGH WRAP AROUND THROW
UKI-WAZA . . . . FLOATING THROW
YOKO-GAKE. . . . . SIDE BODY DROP
YOKO-GURUMA . . . . SIDE WHEEL
YOKO-OTOSHI . . . . SIDE DROP
YOKO-TOMOE-NAGE. . . . . SIDE CIRCLE THROW
YOKO-WAKARE. . . . . SIDE SEPARATION

OSAEKOMI-WAZA   HOLD DOWN TECHNIQUES

KAMI-SHIHO-GATAME. . . . . UPPER FOUR CORNERS HOLD
KATA-GATAME . . . . SHOULDER HOLD
KESA-GATAME. . . . . SCARF HOLD
KUZURE-KAMISHIHO-GATAME. . . . . MODIFIED UPPER FOUR CORNERS HOLD
KUZURE-KESA-GATAME . . . . MODIFIED SCARF HOLD
KUZURE-TATE-SHIHO-GATAME . . . . MODIFIED STRAIGHT FOUR CORNERS HOLD
KUZURE-YOKO-SHIHO-GATAME. . . . . MODIFIED SIDE FOUR CORNERS HOLD
TATE-SHIHO-GATAME. . . . . STRAIGHT FOUR CORNERS HOLD
UKI-GATAME . . . . FLOATING HOLD
USHIRO-KESA-GATAME . . . . REVERSE SCARF HOLD
YOKO-SHIHO-GATAME . . . . SIDE FOUR CORNERS HOLD

SHIME-WAZA   STRANGLING TECHNIQUES

DOJIME (FORBIDDEN) . . . . BODY SCISSORS; TRUNK STRANGLE
GYAKU-JUJI-JIME. . . . . REVERSE CROSS STRANGLE

HADAKA-JIME . . . . NAKED STRANGLE
KATAHA-JIME. . . . . SINGLE WING STRANGLE
KATA-JUJI-JIME . . . . HALF CROSS STRANGLE
KATA-TE-JIME . . . . ONE HAND STRANGLE
NAMI-JUJI-JIME. . . . . NORMAL CROSS STRANGLE
OKURI-ERI-JIME . . . . SLIDING COLLAR STRANGLE
SANKAKU-JIME . . . . TRIANGULAR STRANGLE
SODE-GURUMA-JIME . . . . SLEEVE WHEEL STRANGLE
TSUKKOMI-JIME . . . . THRUSTING STRANGLE
RYOTE-JIME. . . . . TWO HANDED CHOKE

KANSETSU-WAZA   OINT-LOCK TECHNIQUES

ASHI-GARAMI (FORBIDDEN) . . . . LEG ENTANGLEMENT
ASHI-GATAME . . . . LEG ARMLOCK
GYAKU-UDE-GARAMI . . . . REVERSE ENTANGLED ARMLOCK
 HARA-GATAME . . . . STOMACH ARMLOCK
 HIZA-GATAME. . . . . KNEE ARMLOCK
 JUJI-GATAME. . . . . CROSS ARMLOCK
SANKAKU-GATAME . . . . TRIANGULAR ARMLOCK
TE-GATAME . . . . HAND ARMLOCK
UDE-GARAMI. . . . . ENTANGLED ARM LOCK
 UDE-GATAME . . . . STRAIGHT ARM ARMLOCK
 WAKI-GATAME. . . . . ARMPIT ARMLOCK

UKEMI   BREAK-FALLS

ZENPO-UKEMI. . . . . FRONT BREAK-FALL
KOHO-UKEMI. . . . . BACK BREAK-FALL
YOKO-UKEMI . . . . SIDE BREAK-FALL
ZENPO-KAITEN-UKEMI . . . . FORWARD ROLLING BREAK-FALL

KATA   FORMAL EXERCISES

GOSHINJITSU. . . . . FORMS OF SELF-DEFENSE
ITSUTSU-NO-KATA. . . . . FORMS OF FIVE
JUNO-KATA . . . . FORMS OF GENTLENESS
KATAME-NO-KATA. . . . . FORMS OF GRAPPLING
KIME-NO-KATA. . . . . FORMS OF DECISION
KOSHIKI-NO-KATA. . . . . FORMS OF ANTIQUE
NAGE-NO-KATA . . . . FORMS OF THROWING

MISCELLANEOUS

ATEMI-WAZA . . . . STRIKING TECHNIQUES
KAESHI-WAZA . . . . COUNTER TECHNIQUES
KATAME-WAZA. . . . . ALL GRAPPLING TECHNIQUES
NAGE-WAZA. . . . . THROWING TECHNIQUES
NEWAZA . . . . GRAPPLING TECHNIQUES (NON STANDING)
RENRAKU-WAZA. . . . . COMBINATION TECHNIQUES
RENZOKU-WAZA . . . . CONTINUOUS COMBINATION
 . . . . OF TECHNIQUES
TACHI-WAZA . . . . THROWS EXECUTED FROM STANDING

Printed in Great Britain
by Amazon